TO

Ruoam K. Bga

IS 41.13

The Book on Bullies: Break Free in Forty (40 Minutes or 40 Days)

Includes Forty Devotionals to Fortify Your Soul

Susan K. Boyd MS, LMFT
Licensed Marriage & Family Therapist

WESTBOW
PRESS®
A DIVISION OF THOMAS NELSON
& ZONDERVAN

WestBow Press books may be ordered through booksellers or by contacting:

WestBow Press
A Division of Thomas Nelson & Zondervan
1663 Liberty Drive
Bloomington, IN 47403
www.westbowpress.com
1 (866) 928-1240

Because of the dynamic nature of the Internet, any web addresses or
links contained in this book may have changed since publication and
may no longer be valid. The views expressed in this work are solely those
of the author and do not necessarily reflect the views of the publisher,
and the publisher hereby disclaims any responsibility for them.

Any people depicted in stock imagery provided by Thinkstock are
models, and such images are being used for illustrative purposes only.
Certain stock imagery © Thinkstock.

ISBN: 978-1-5127-9606-3 (sc)
ISBN: 978-1-5127-9607-0 (hc)
ISBN: 978-1-5127-9605-6 (e)

Library of Congress Control Number: 2017910998

Print information available on the last page.

WestBow Press rev. date: 8/10/2017

No more fear of threatening sounds
Or the unexpected strike,
I will go Christ's way,
Find my path, and live my life.

To my mom, Florence Ellen Hoffman McClusky
She inspired me with her strength of character, love of
God, family and desire for excellence. I will always be
grateful she encouraged me to write. I miss her every day.

Cyberbullying!
In Chapter # 7
Avoid Traps

CONTENTS

PART I—STRATEGIES

PART II—DAILY DEVOTIONALS

PREFACE

THE SECRET

I would like to tell you a secret. You will not believe it, as you have not yet experienced it, because you are discouraged and tired. How could you not be? You have been criticized, teased, manipulated, or threatened. Emotionally and maybe even physically, you have been beaten down. And it continues.

Every day you get up, you feel a little sick. The mean words travel around in your head and the hurtful pictures flash across your mind. There are times you don't want to go anywhere, or else you just want to run away, all because you are being bullied.

For just a moment, I want to imagine I can time travel. I am finding every client I ever counseled who was a victim of bullies. I am handing him or her this book while he or she is still in the throes of the battle. I am encouraging him or her, "Read every chapter slowly. Write all your thoughts, feelings, and strategies at the end of each chapter in your personal inventory and plan of action!" Then I share my secret with him or her. But he or she won't believe it. Not yet.

Once you take this book as your own survival guide and tactical manual, you will be prepared and ready to break free from any bullies who come after you. Why is there scripture in a book on bullies? If you are, in fact, made in your creator's image, then who knows better what you need to gain your greatest victory in your darkest moments? By having access to God's strength, wisdom, insight, and heart, no one can stop you for long. You are a reflection of the God that made you. If you look to him for your future and not be shortsighted or blindsided by bullies, you will see a new vision!

That vision includes a path that becomes a road to freedom and to all you will be able to do. Bullies don't want you to see you have a future. They bothered you today, but don't lose heart about what will happen tomorrow. I wrote *The Book on Bullies*, but you are writing *The Book on You*, and that is a wonderful story that only you can write! The secret I hope you will believe is this, "Your story is not over."

ACKNOWLEDGMENTS

The value of any book depends on how important it is in the reader's life. Books can inform, entertain, or cause the reader to think, feel, or move in new directions. I want to thank friends and family who believed in me, and the potential power of this book, to help those who have suffered at the hands of bullies. They prayed for me and asked me to write and expound on the Break Free Method from my first book. They gave me a reason to write from my heart, to brave people being bullied every day.

Thank you to my granddaughter for her excellent advice, "Put more quotes in your second book ... I like quotes ... and put more chocolate chips in your cookies." She was absolutely right on both accounts. The book is better for it, and so are the cookies. Thank you also to my grandson for helping me with the inspirational and encouraging music in the resource section of this book.

A big thank you to Tanna and Jan, who both promoted, donated, and recommended my first book much more than I did. Thank you to Jerry, Judi, Charlie, Emily, Dale, and Tanna for taking the time to read several of the devotionals in this book, Erica for some editing advice and thanks to Deb for all of her encouragement in the writing of this book.

Thank you to Bob Dutko who inspired me to write more about the three types of bullies, after having me on his Nationally Syndicated Radio Program, to discuss my first Book on Bullies. And to all my friends who gave out books to those who needed them the most, thank you.

Last, and most important of all, I want to thank the one who suffered the most at the hands of bullies. He was broken for us and buried, but he could not be kept down. A risen Savior knows how to give power to those who look to him for hope and a future. Thank you, Lord Jesus, for all the stories and scripture, that teach us what it means be kind, to be strong, and to be yours.

INTRODUCTION

I wrote *The Book on Bullies: How to Handle Them Without Becoming One of Them* in 2012. It has been used in churches and organizations. It has been used with kids, teenagers in juvenile hall, adults in Bible studies, Christian school in-service for teachers, and family meetings, to name a few. I have been thrilled to know that little book became a manual for the individual as well as a group study guide in addressing the important issue of bullying. I was interviewed on national radio simply because this subject affects so many families.

This second book, *The Book on Bullies: Break Free in Forty (40 Minutes or 40 Days)*, was written specifically to the person being bullied. It is meant to be an important tool in the hands of kids, teenagers, and adults facing daily abuse from bullies. The newest changes in the definition of bullying, the most current laws, research, and resources available, will be at your fingertips.

This book is your personal GPS, helping you to navigate when you are deep inside the bully's world. You need to know specific and clear direction to get out of a situation, where your safe places are, and the fastest way to get there. Forty minutes is the best scenario, but forty days also gives you an end point. Bullying has to come to an end. And just as your GPS knows when you are going the wrong way and may tell you to recalculate, the devotionals here offer a fresh way of thinking, a new map using scripture to lead you where you want to go.

The power in this book, as with the last text, is in the resources drawn from books of the Bible. *The Book on Bullies: Break Free in Forty* also incorporates examples from daily life and my years of experience as a therapist helping individuals break free from bullies. The Break Free Method was originally introduced in my first book; however, this newest book is my answer to those who want more specific strategies on how to put that method into practice for themselves.

The Break Free Method is divided into chapters, using the alliteration of "Break Free" in part I to find your way out of being bullied and break loose from bullies. The devotionals in part II are there to fortify you for the next forty days. Read one devotional each day for your quiet time as you work through your book. The devotional reading is your private moment of reflection and refreshment.

Using Christian principles, which are threaded through out this book, again, as in the previous book, does not mean the contents apply only for Christians. This text is a handbook for anyone wanting freedom from bullies. If you or someone you care about needs tools now and has the desire to find wisdom that can be found in scripture, then it is time to get started with *The Book on Bullies: Break Free in Forty*!

BREAK FREE METHOD

B = **B**e bold, not timid.
R = **R**ecognize your strengths.
E = **E**mpower yourself; find and use your voice.
A = **A**void traps.
K = **K**eep your distance.

F = **F**orgive bullies; don't trust bullies.
R = **R**efuse to be intimidated.
E = **E**nlist help and support.
E = **E**valuate your life goals and live them.

PART I
Strategies

A strategy is only useful when you know it, believe it, and use it.

CHAPTER 1

Bullying: Definitions, Laws, and Programs

Peace is not absence of conflict, but handling conflict by a peaceful means.

—Ronald Reagan

You recognize bullies when you see them if you have been their target. You know the helpless feeling. You never forget that. But if this type of abuse is going to be stopped, a clear, definitive picture of bullying is necessary for schools and other settings.

My first book on bullying, *The Book on Bullies: How to Handle Them Without Becoming One of Them*, begins with a definition drawn from Dictionary.com. It states that a bully is "a blustering, quarrelsome, overbearing person, who habitually badgers and intimidates smaller or weaker people." This is still a workable, descriptive definition. However, similar definitions, some with more detail, have surfaced in the research and legislative material.

The definition of bullying in the United States has changed over time and differs slightly according to states, organizations, and institutional interpretations of that word. It will most likely continue to evolve. But certain traits remain the same in most descriptions. For instance, Dr. Daniel Olweus came up with a widely used definition. It stresses three components: aggressive behaviors that are repeated and involve a power imbalance favoring the perpetrator. The victim is also not able to defend against the negative behaviors of one or more of the perpetrators.[1]

The Centers for Disease Control and Prevention (CDC) believes that, for the sake of research and information gathering, a uniform definition is important. Its findings and conclusions can be found in its report *Bullying Surveillance among Youths: Uniform Definitions for Public Health and Recommended Data Elements (1–101)*. Its definition of bullying among youths is as follows:

> Bullying is any unwanted aggressive behavior(s) by another youth or group of youths who are not siblings or current dating partners that involves an observed or perceived power imbalance and is repeated multiple times or is highly likely to be repeated. Bullying may inflict harm or

distress on the targeted youth including physical, psychological, social, or educational harm.

The CDC also focuses on two modes of bullying and three types of bullying among youths.

MODES OF BULLYING

- Direct: aggressive behaviors that occur in the presence of the targeted youth
- Indirect: aggressive behaviors that are not directly communicated to the targeted youth, such as rumors

TYPES OF BULLYING

- Physical: includes hitting, kicking, punching, spitting, tripping, and pushing
- Verbal: includes oral or written communication by the perpetrator who causes the targeted youth harm
  - Examples include taunts, name-calling, threatening or offensive written notes or hand gestures, inappropriate sexual comments, or verbal threats.
- Relational: includes, but is not limited to, efforts to isolate the targeted youth by keeping him or her from interacting with peers
  - Indirect relational bullying includes spreading false or harmful rumors, publicly writing derogatory comments, or posting embarrassing images in a physical or electronic space, without the targeted youth's permission or knowledge.[2]

Biblically speaking, bullying goes back as far as Cain and Abel in the book of Genesis, if you assume Cain bullied Abel before actually murdering him. Cain killed his brother out of anger and jealousy. God tried to warn Cain to shift his perspective and control his temper before it led him into violence. Cain would not listen (Gen. 4:5–12). Later in the book of Genesis, Ishmael mocked his little half-brother Isaac so badly that Rebecca wanted her stepson and his mom out of their camp (Gen. 21:8–10). The list goes on, not only in the Bible but in everyday life as well.

Bullying behavior has been around since the beginning of time and will continue. But the alarming rate of children committing suicide because they were bullied, and mass shootings at schools by alleged victims of bullies (bully-victims), has not always been around. Fortunately in the past few years, our government and schools have decided to do something about bullying. They've chosen to protect children and teenagers as well as, in some circumstances, adults by antibullying legislation.

After the school shootings on April 20, 1999, at Columbine High School, where the student perpetrators allegedly were victims of bullying, the media spotlight began to shine on this subject. However, as in many cases of retaliation, lots of the victims of the Columbine shooters were innocent of bullying anyone. Other school shootings have followed in a like pattern, with many of the shooters claiming acts of revenge against their bullies.

News reports have covered several suicides by children and teenagers who could not stand the cruel attacks their peers made upon them on and off campus. The abuse was physical, emotional, and sometimes indirect, such as cyberbullying (bullying through an electronic communication, usually done anonymously). Posting cruel pictures, words, and accusations has ruined reputations and held the targeted up to ridicule. Unfortunately cyberbullies have had a long reach to a huge, gullible audience with little danger of being caught. That is changing as law enforcement becomes more technologically savvy.

All fifty states in the United States have passed school and antibullying legislation, the first being Georgia in 1999. Montana was the last state, passing antibullying legislation in 2015. There are also watchdog organizations like Bully Police USA advocating for and reporting on various antibullying legislation.[3]

Some of the legislative changes that have arisen at the state level in regard to bullying also have the expectation that schools will implement antibullying programs. Some newer legislation addresses cyberbullying. For instance, in 2008, California passed a law directly related to cyberbullying. It gave school administrators authority to discipline students for bullying others offline or online. In 2013, California clarified the role of schools in bullying cases that originate away from school. It stated, "'Electronic act' means the creation and transmission originated on or off the school site"[4] Illinois enacted similar legislation on August 1, 2015.[5]

On July 11, 2011, Hawaii signed into law consequences for the adults in charge of minors who bully. Parents and guardians share the responsibility for bullying. The law states, "The child's guardian or parent may be fined $100.00 per offense."[6] Louisiana made its fines to be "no more than $500.00 and imprisonment for not more than 6 months or both."[7] Maine defines cyberbullying as "injurious hazing."[8]

On July 1, 2014, Minnesota covered quite a bit of ground in its legislation, with a definition of cyberbullying.

> "Cyber-bullying" means bullying using technology or other electronic communication, including, but not limited to a transfer of a sign, signal, writing, image, sound or data, including a post on a social network Internet web site or forum, transmitted through a computer, cell phone, or other electronic device.[9]

The Safe and Drug-Free Schools and Communities Act is part of the No Child Left Behind Act of 2001. It provides federal support to promote school safety but does not specifically address bullying and harassment in schools. Presently no federal laws deal directly with school bullying.[10] Bullying may, however, trigger responsibilities under one or more of the federal antidiscrimination laws enforced by the United States Department of Education's Office for Civil Rights.

For instance, California Anti-Bullying Laws and Policies lists these groups to be covered under California Harassment Law, as federal law requires schools that receive federal funding to address discrimination. These categorizations can be found in the list below.

- disability
- gender
- nationality
- race or ethnicity
- religion
- sexual orientation
- association with a person or group with one or more of these actual or perceived characteristics[11]

Some controversy surrounds the government's ability to stop school bullying. The National School Safety and Security Services question the motive behind some antibullying legislation. They are concerned the line between "feel-good legislation" and "meaningful legislation" is not clear. They state,

> Anti-bullying legislation, typically an unfunded mandate, requiring schools to have anti-bullying policies but providing no financial resources to improve school climate and security, offer more political hype than substance for helping school administration address the problem.[12]

Another part of the controversy is accountability. Each state draws up its own laws to address bullying. While expanding requirements for schools and passing new legislation, there are few, if any, formal procedures to audit schools' policies or provide the technical support and guidance. Furthermore, few systematic studies demonstrate if antibullying laws and policies are reducing bullying.[13]

Some researchers are questioning whether the antibullying programs actually work. *US News & World Report* cites a study in the *Journal of Criminology* that says students in schools with antibullying initiatives are actually more likely to be victims of bullying than students in schools without such programs. Seokjin Jeong, lead author of that research, points out that the programs may help students learn what a bully does and looks like, teaching them how to better hide their behaviors.[14] Jeong and his coauthor, Byung Hyun Lee, suggest systemic changes in the schools, such as employing guards, using metal detectors, and conducting bag and locker searches.[15]

An alternative approach to prevent bullying may be to change the culture within the school. Stuart Twemlow, a professor of health sciences at University College in London and coauthor of *Preventing Bullying and School Violence*, supports this idea. He states, "The bullies are not the cause of the problem. They are the result of the problem. The problem is the climate of the school." He further states, "When you have a lot of bullies at a school, you have a problem with the leadership of the school. And that's complicated."[16]

Affecting school climate by changing norms and tolerance for bullying within the student population may be one of the answers to prevention. Nancy Willard, MS, JD, is author of *Influencing Positive Peer Interventions: A Synthesis of the Research Insight*. In it, she discussed a framework for Embrace Civility in the Digital Age, a bullying prevention program, Be a Friend-Lend a Hand.

Willard's conclusions, after reviewing the research, were that a high social status student who moves to defend someone who is being bullied or attempts to stop a bully would be admired and that other students would copy that behavior. However, if the bully is of high social status and the target is of low social status, other students are less likely to intervene for fear they would also be viewed as lower in status.[17]

Therefore, three strategies would be pursued through the Be a Friend-Lend a Hand Program. Not surprisingly, these are empowering the high status students; increasing the ranks of defenders by lowering the social status barrier; and undermining the status of those who engage in aggression.[18]

The Expect Respect program also focuses on changing the culture by encouraging the targeted and witnesses to tell the bully to stop and walk away so they provide no additional attention to the bully. I also recommend this in my book, *The Book on Bullies: How to Handle Them without Becoming One of Them.*

Stan Davis' book, *Empowering Bystanders in Bullying Prevention,* gives many examples of strategies teachers can use in addressing bullying.[19] Finally the International Institute for Restorative Practices recommends questions that witnesses can ask bullies to help them rethink and possibly change their behavior.[20]

Many schools now have Be Kind Clubs, or clubs with different names but similar goals. These student groups put on short skits for their school or other schools with anti-bullying themes as well as promoting Good Samaritan type projects. Getting kids involved in the solution may be the best remedy for the problem.

So now you are more familiar with state laws, research, and some of the programs being recommended or used to curtail bullying. Read the definition of bullying that will be used in this book and a brief overview of the program I have designed specifically for you to break free from bullies.

Remember, even though different states and institutions are continually drafting variations of the meaning of bullying, their definitions are nevertheless similar. The following three elements (as previously mentioned in Dr. Olweus' basic description) make up the most solid definition for this book. Bullying is:

- aggressive behavior (whether verbal, physical, written, or electronically communicated);
- repeated abuse (or the likelihood it will be repeated, for example, a threat made); and
- an imbalance of power in favor of the perpetrator.

If any of the three factors in the bully definition are not part of the behavior, it is not bullying. For example, fighting between two people is not necessarily bullying. It does not meet the definition if they are both initiating the aggression and no one is simply defending himself or herself. It is not bullying if there is no power imbalance (one is not smaller or weaker mentally, physically, nor disadvantaged, for example, by gossip or inappropriate photos being spread across the Internet without the other person's permission). Bullying is not a single episode unless there is an ongoing threat that it will probably happen again.

Some agencies and institutions only recognize bullying as between children or adolescents, that are not siblings, and only at or directly after school. Others, however, for instance, Ontario and Alberta, have identified bullying between adults as well and implemented anti-bullying laws to include workplace bullying in 2012.[21]

I believe that bullying can go on between people of all ages in a variety of situations, for example, children and teenagers in school or neighborhoods, among adults in the workplace or teenagers on a work site, as well as family members behind closed doors, to name a few. That is why my first book, *The Book on Bullies: How to Handle Them Without Becoming One of Them*, and now, my second book, *The Book on Bullies: Break Free in Forty (Forty Minutes or Forty Days)* is intended to be used by or for children, adolescents, and adults.

I have written both books with the hope that people of all ages would read or be read to, sharing this information with one another in group discussions, senior high or youth groups, adult and youth Bible studies, or around the dinner table. An individual eleven to a hundred years old will find most of the information in both my books on bullies usable. (For example, my granddaughter was eleven years old when she picked up my first book on her own and read it cover to cover!) That is my goal, to get help in the hands and minds of those who want it and encourage them to share with one another. That way, no one will ever have to suffer alone in secret at the hands of bullies.

How can reading *The Book on Bullies: Break Free in Forty* help you stop the bullies? This is your own self-help program designed for you and your personal use! Each chapter gives you a different strategy to try from the Break Free Method. Several chapters have a very short list of questions. You choose and mark one of two answers. Add up your score.

Now you will know (maybe for the first time) your strengths and weaknesses. Bullies prey on your weaknesses and back down from your strengths. The rest of the chapters give ideas and scriptures you can apply to your own situation. After you read each chapter, you can journal or strategize in the sections called "My Personal Inventory" and "My Plan of Action."

Use the forty devotionals (as mentioned in the introduction) found in part II as soon as you start reading this book. Read one devotional every day to empower yourself for the next forty days. The devotionals are meant to inspire, uplift, and fortify you against bullies while you grow closer to your creator. Bullying can make you forget who you are and take away all sense of purpose and self-worth. This book is designed to bring you confidently back to yourself; meanwhile, bullies lose their grip on your life!

What new information did you learn about bullying that helps you?

What is new or hopeful to you about the different laws according to states' interpretation?

What kind of program would you like to see implemented in your school or workplace to stop bullies?

Do you see bullies where you work or go to school? How are they bullying others?

Are you being bullied?

What are you hoping to find in this book to help you break free from bullies?

Are you willing to read this book and try out the tests so you can hopefully be empowered to break free from bullies? Circle one:

Yes   No

Will you try to write on your personal inventory and your plan of action at the end of each chapter? (You will be more prepared to break free from your bullies in forty minutes or forty days!)

Yes   No

Would you be willing to give this book to someone being bullied?

Yes   No

MY PLAN OF ACTION

CHAPTER 2

Bully Types: Narcissistic Bullies, Backdoor Bullies, and Crowd Pleaser Bullies

I, wisdom, dwell together with prudence; I possess knowledge and discretion.

—Proverbs 8:12

Wouldn't it be helpful to identify different types of bullies when they begin to harass you? That is what this chapter is all about. I have noticed throughout my years of counseling in my private practice that people who perpetually bully others fall into one or more of three categories: narcissistic bullies, backdoor bullies, and the crowd pleaser bullies. I first coined these terms, introduced in chapters 1 through 3, with specific examples from scripture in *The Book on Bullies: How to Handle Them Without Becoming One of Them*.[1] Readers of my first book asked me to expound more on these three bullies and how to deal with them. So here is more detailed information on these bully types. This is the way to spot them and a way to stop them.

Keep in mind that any of us can be guilty of bullying at any time, if we are not considerate or compassionate. But those who pick on people on a regular basis are not unintentionally bullying. They are bullies. Allen Kurzweil, the best-selling author, wrote a book about his forty-year search for his twelve-year-old bully. He wanted to see if his bully had changed or if he were still victimizing people in some way or another. His book, *The Whipping Boy*, shows how deep the emotional scars go, how long they can last, and what can oftentimes be the result of this behavior for the bullied and the bully.[2]

One longitudinal study looked at the effects of bullying. The results highlighted that childhood bullies were more likely to engage in risky or illegal behaviors in adulthood. Bullies were more likely to be convicted of felonies, abuse drugs, and be poorer and lonelier than their former victims.[3] Research cited by the stopbulllying.gov website states that many kids who bully grow up to be adults with convictions and traffic citations and continue to bully others.[4]

People can have a change of heart and stop abusive, relentless aggression. But while they habitually victimize others, they need to be recognized. When you can identify their bullying methods, you can break free from their abuse.

The narcissistic bullies fall into the first category of bully types. They are very self-serving with a sense of self-importance. The term "narcissism" originated in Greek mythology. The legend goes that a handsome young god named Narcissus was walking by a lake or riverbank, bent down to get a drink, and was surprised and enthralled by the handsome face looking back at him from the water. He fell in love with himself and became entranced with his own reflection. When he could not obtain the object of his desire, he died by the water's edge.[5]

So with this myth of Narcissus in mind, you probably understand that narcissistic people are in love with themselves and need others to give them the attention and respect that they are dying to have, whenever possible. Narcissistic people have difficulty understanding or even wanting to understand why everyone would not want to admire them, listen to them, and drink in their essence.

Now imagine what happens when narcissists becomes bullies. What do you have? Narcissistic bullies can be charming, fun, and even disarming. They appear happy, if you listen to them and agree with them. In other words, they expect to see their reflection in your eyes. If, however, you ever disagree with them and fail to give them the admiration they crave, they can turn on you with a vengeance. They feel shame when you fail to admire and appreciate their greatness. So to alleviate this horrible feeling, they shame and disrespect you until they feel powerful again.

Narcissistic bullies lack empathy and won't care they are hurting you. They may pin you against a wall and make you sit and listen while they lecture or belittle you. They frequently go off on a tirade, scream, make fun of you, humiliate, or physically accost you until you break down. But even then, they may not stop verbal or physical abuse until their anxiety subsides and their release of anger is finished.

If narcissistic bullies had a slogan, it would probably be one you have heard that says, "I am not arguing with you. I am just explaining to you why I am right." or "Think I am sarcastic?

Watch me pretend to care!" The college professor, an avowed atheist, in the movie *God Is Not Dead* was a perfect example of this narcissistic bully.

The teacher targeted a young Christian man in his philosophy class because he would not agree that God did not exist. At one point, the teacher makes the statement, "In this class I am God." The professor challenged his student to defend his view before the class. As the student made his case each day, he began to win over the professor's other students. The teacher became enraged, a natural narcissistic reaction. This is the reality of confronting narcissists. If they lose an argument, it is tantamount to losing face, which spells shame in the realm of narcissistic bullies.

Now that you understand a little bit of how narcissistic people think and how narcissistic bullies act, how can this help you in dealing with them? First, remember what motivates the bullying. These bullies need to put you down to feel they are up on top. Being superior or special is like oxygen to narcissists. They don't believe they can survive without it. Knowing this gives you keys to escape their bullying tactics.

One key to stopping their bad behavior lies in knowing how to confront them. The following are a few phrases that often stop or slow down the narcissistic bullies. You need to show them they can't put you down. Use "I" language instead of starting a remark with "you." "You" can sound like an attack, as if you are calling the bullies names or ordering them around. But starting the statement with "I" indicates an ownership of your opinion and your right to say it. When the bullying begins, turn to them, look them in the eye, and say any one of the following:

- "If I did something to you, tell me. Otherwise, stop!"
- "I don't deserve that, so I'm not going to take it."
- "I am not disrespecting you, so don't disrespect me!"

Another key to freeing yourself from these bullies, which is also useful in battling most bullies, is to simply ignore them. Avoid eye contact and make no expression, so it appears you don't hear them. It is hard to pick a fight with someone who won't even acknowledge that there is a fight. Move away and keep going to wherever you planned to be. It is difficult to hit a moving target. Don't stick around and take abuse of any kind.

The narcissistic bullies are pretty easy to spot now that you know how they operate. The backdoor bullies, however, are more difficult to recognize as they often act friendly. They may be friends, colleagues, confidants, or they may even be members of your family. They do lots of harm by camouflaging their hurtful behavior with humor or behind your back. This is why they are called backdoor bullies. They come at the bullying in subtle ways, through the backdoor of your relationship.

Backdoor bullies hurt you with sarcastic remarks (which they disguise as "I was just kidding") in private or sometimes in front of others to discredit you. But more often, they harm you without you knowing until later. One of their tactics is their use of information.

If you confide in backdoor bullies, you may discover that they told others your secret in order to embarrass you. This is not a slip or accident. It is very intentional and keeps happening. Remember, even with backdoor bullies, all three parts of bullying must be present for this to be true bullying: Words or behaviors will be aggressive. The bullying continues to happen, and there is an imbalance in power in favor of the perpetrator. In this case, subtle undermining becomes their power. They will also misquote you, take one part of your statement out of context, or exaggerate the intensity with which it was said in order to hurt your relationship with others. It can then sound as if you were spreading vicious gossip instead of a casual remark.

Another tactic of backdoor bullies is the way they take advantage of you. If you are a student, they copy your homework, try to get you to do their assignments, or cheat on tests, looking at your answers. If you are a teenager or adult on the job, your backdoor bully typically makes you look bad by taking credit for your accomplishments or blaming you for problems that come up at work. You end up doing their job when they slack off.

Sometimes backdoor bullies are people in a position of power such as a supervisor, someone with more seniority, or a group leader in a group project at school or on the job. Because they are in charge, they make and change rules however and whenever it is convenient for them. If you question them about their unfair practices they will probably tag you for retaliation, telling themselves you are challenging their authority.

If backdoor bullies get angry, they will probably not confront you directly, but talk about you behind your back, say snide remarks, roll their eyes when in your presence or find a way to hurt you later. This is how they differ from the narcissistic bullies, who are more likely to fly into a rage as soon as they are irritated or decide to target you. If the backdoor bullies wore T-shirts, they would probably have slogans across their chests saying, "I don't get mad; I get even."

So how do you confront these bullies in order to handle and stop them? Unlike the narcissistic bullies who overtly bully you and feel justified and unconcerned who sees it, these culprits do not like being shown up in public. Remember, they do all their dirty work behind the scenes. They want people to see you in a bad light, but not be shown up for what they have been saying or doing in the shadows.

The good news is that backdoor bullies are easier to reason with than the narcissistic bullies. But first you will need to confront them with their behavior. Here are a few ways to do that. These declarations can make the backdoor bullies realize you know what they have been doing to you and you expect them to stop, or else you will keep calling them out with the facts. Choose any one of these that apply to your situation when bullying occurs, and note, once again, these also start with "I":

- "I don't think I deserve that remark you just made."
- "I am not sharing my homework or answers with anyone."
- "I am doing my work, not yours."
- "Just for the record, this is what I just said, and this is what I just heard you say."
- "I don't know anything about him." (Use this statement if they are pumping you for information about someone else.) "You need to ask him if you have questions."

A last recommendation when addressing backdoor bullies: keep standing up to them when you are sure you have the facts, or get the facts, so they have to stop the bullying or be shown up for it. Remember the narcissistic bullies get angry and react with a knee-jerk type reflex, but backdoor bullies plot and deny. Getting the goods on them lets them and anyone else involved know that they can't pretend they are not bullying and get away with it.

The last category of bully types is the one that most of us think of when we hear the word "bully." It is Biff who torments and teases poor George McFly in the *Back to the Future* movies. He fits right in with this group, the crowd pleaser bullies.

These bullies, whether running in packs or by themselves, relish the opportunity to humiliate their victims in front of others. It is all a show to impress peers, who may be coworkers, classmates, friends, or even gang members. But it is a marathon exhibition of degrading others to get the attention the bullies crave. If these abusive braggarts can make others feel and appear helpless, they imagine they themselves look powerful.

Crowd pleaser bullies need someone to watch them perform. That is why one of the best moves bystanders can make, is to refuse to be entertained by the abuse. When there is no audience, these bullies lose interest. They hope their caustic behavior will bring them popularity. If they had tattoos, they would read, "Be afraid. Be very afraid" or "Bad to the Bone." They want the reputation of being "the bad men on campus" or the "mean girls."

Tactics to stop these bullies vary. The best countermeasure to their showing off is to ignore them. They want a reaction from you of shock, fear, groveling, or begging for mercy. If crowd pleaser bullies are singling you out, give them no attention and leave the scene.

If you have to confront crowd pleaser bullies when they are in the act of bullying, it is best to do it with a crowd of your own, as there is safety in numbers. Travel in groups. Showing off and putting pressure on you is harder when the people around are your friends.

Another option, if the bullying is not physical but verbal attacks, is to talk to this bully later alone, without the attention of the crowd. Tell him or her that you want the bullying to stop as it hurts your feelings. Sometimes this gets through to crowd pleaser bullies. With no audience to impress and your willingness to be vulnerable by admitting it hurts, you are challenging their belief system to shift from "I was just playing with you" to "I really harmed you." You are taking the chance that this information will be used against you in the next bout of public bullying. But the fact that you showed respect, talking confidentially, may gain you respect, and the bullying might stop.

If the bullying continues and you are caught off guard and have to deal with these bullies, stand up tall and use as few words as necessary, acting as if their bullying does not really affect you. No matter what you said in private to crowd pleaser bullies, once you are on display for their enjoyment, it is time to deflect everything being thrown at you. If you show any weakness publicly with these bullies, the bullying will just get worse. They are like sharks that smell blood in the water. They can go into a feeding frenzy, honing in on your embarrassment, if they suspect they have made you look foolish in front of others. Stay calm, protect yourself, and get out of there.

If you handle yourself well in front of bystanders, the bullies' status goes down, and yours comes up, which makes it uncomfortable for crowd pleaser bullies to get the popularity they want. The braver and less concerned you sound, the higher your status will go, and the lower the bullies' will fall. When these bullies can't find your fear or weakness, the fun stops. When that happens, the bullying may stop as well.

Unlike the specific and narrow statements you make to backdoor bullies, you need to do just the opposite when crowd pleaser bullies are harassing you. Your remarks need to be vague. These bullies will make demeaning remarks about your looks, intelligence, personality, family, and so forth. Don't get into a sparring match of words. Then they know they got to you. Instead use words that give them nowhere to go. Pick one response from the following list and fire it back when cruel remarks are aimed at you:

- "Whatever!"
- "Don't care."
- "Yeah, right."
- "Uh-huh."
- "Hmm."
- (Yawn and stretch)
- "Boring."
- "Don't think so."
- "Gotta go!"

Note: You want to look cool, calm, and disinterested when you give your reply.

Make your remarks and then make your exit. When you go where you want to go, do what you want to do, and ignore all the cutting remarks or physical pranks that crowd pleaser bullies try to play on you, they lose their audience and their victim. Then the show is over!

As you understand all three types of bullies discussed in this chapter, you undermine their power over you. These are not people bullying you. These are bullies with an agenda and a pattern. The victims change, but the perpetrators remain the same. Hopefully now you have a plan and a list of tactical strategies to stop being one of those victims. Use your personal inventory and plan of action following this chapter to help you process this information and write your own plan into action.

Which bully types have you noticed the most where you work, live, or go to school?

What type or types of bullies have tried to bully you?

Write down the responses you are going to try with the bullies the next time they pick on you.

Name some strategies you have already tried. Did they work? Why or why not?

Pick a bully type for which you want to be prepared. Now take a few minutes and start writing in your plan of action. Write anything you will say or do to break free of their bullying.

MY PLAN OF ACTION

CHAPTER 3
Why the Number Forty?

Character cannot be developed in ease and quiet. Only through experience of trial and suffering can the soul be strengthened, ambition inspired, success achieved.

—Helen Keller

You now know more about the definitions, laws, and programs relating to bullying after reading chapter 1. Chapter 2 helped you understand the type of bullies you are probably up against. But whether you are an adult in a toxic work setting, a student just trying to get through the day, or someone in an abusive relationship, you need a plan of attack of your own. This is not retaliation so you can bully back. These are decisive strategies to stop the aggression aimed at you. But you will need an offensive and defensive plan if you are going to have success.

Let's use a football analogy for a moment in order to understand this principle. A winning football coach designs the playbook that the team puts into practice. Then by understanding the opponent's typical plays on the field, the coach works on both the offensive and defensive plan to win, not to simply stop losing. A coach always wants the team to see themselves as winners with a vision of going all the way to the end zone. Defense alone will never win the game. Stopping the aggressors by putting a defensive plan into play while also taking the offense to move the ball by touchdowns, field goals, and sometimes ten yards at a time gets the ball across the goal line.

Bullying stops when two things happen in your life: you move forward, and bullies move back. Both movements need to take place. If bullies don't stop you will be harmed either emotionally, physically, or both. If you don't move forward, for fear of being bullied, you will remain afraid and shrink back from life or be enraged and become a bully yourself.

So you need an end point. There has to be a goal line somewhere. This answers the question: why forty? Forty has significance in scripture in the Old and New Testaments. Both forty days and forty years marked special events and time periods in the lives of people of faith. Forty minutes is the more optimal choice for immediately handling or reporting bullying and having it stop. But realistically, you may find even after you report it to someone or confront bullies that the process may go closer to forty days than forty minutes. So this book will help you every step of the way between that forty minutes and forty days. Many of God's people in the Bible suffered forty years or longer. However, I don't think anyone wants to wait forty years for the bullying to stop, though that has unfortunately been the case for some individuals and families that have come to me for help.

A person can only stand so much torment. How do you survive it, and how can you stop it? Analyzing bullying from a scriptural point of view brings historical and spiritual weight to the subject as well as applications for today. Before focusing on the Break Free Method in part I (chapters 3 through 12), or the forty daily devotionals in part II, read briefly about three very different situations where forty days became instrumental in God's plan for breaking free from bullies.

NOAH

We only have to look at the first book in the Bible, Genesis, to find the greatest number of bullies on earth. Genesis 6–8 marks the place in history when the world was so depraved and people were so vicious that it broke God's heart. Genesis 6:5–9:

> The Lord saw how great man's wickedness on earth had become, and that every inclination of the thoughts of his heart was only evil all the time. The Lord was grieved that he had made man on the earth, and his heart was filled with pain. So the Lord said, "I will wipe out mankind, whom I have created, from the face of the earth-men and animals, and creatures that move along the ground, and birds of the air-for I am grieved that I have made them." But Noah found favor in the eyes of God. Noah was a righteous man, blameless among the people of his time, and he walked faithfully with God.

God told Noah to build an ark. So Noah obeyed and worked, constructing every board and dowel to the exact specifications of God's design. For seven days, the world watched without repenting. Noah's neighbors must have been curious and no doubt laughed and ridiculed him for building a boat to withstand a storm and flood when they had never even seen rain. Bullies don't believe you have the means to get away from them.

Noah's story is proof that God grieves over cruelty and sees when his children suffer because of it. It is also evidence that he can provide the way of escape. After Noah and his family had taken two of each type of animal into the ark, at God's careful instruction, and gathered food they would need for the journey, the giant door slammed shut.

For forty days and nights, Noah; his family, including his sons and their wives; and the animals listened as the rain pounded onto their rooftop. Torrents of rain poured from the sky, while underground springs broke through the earth's crust, gushing like fountains and geysers. The noise from the storm—possibly thunder, gales of wind, and falling buildings and trees—and the inability to see outside might have kept them from hearing and seeing what was happening to the others. As the water began to rise and lift their boat, floating it away, the people outside perished. Noah and his family, however, experienced God's love that held them in the palm of his hand.

How many years had Noah suffered living with the most violent society in the world's history? How did he keep from being corrupted himself? Genesis 6:9: "Noah was a righteous man, blameless among the people of his time and he walked with God."

Sometimes God will be your only ally in your world of bullies. Noah lived with it for years. When God decided the whole world would be destroyed, he protected his faithful. God gave Noah the design and measurements. Noah got to work, believing one day the bullying would be over and he would be gone.

God will show you a way out of the madness around you. Keep

walking with him. Study him. You do this by reading scripture every day, which is the way he talks to you. And pray, which is simply you talking to him. Take the next forty days and find a time each day when you shut yourself up with God (so to speak). Get your attention off those who have made your life so miserable, and remember this is your time to look to the future. Like Noah in the hull of that ship, you may be tossed around, but you are leaving the worst behind you.

Think how daunting the voyage was for Noah. Can you imagine days of shoveling poop and trying to confine it to one area of the ark, feeding and separating animals, and attending to people who were getting seasick? He had to keep up the morale of his family so they would not become afraid or discouraged. Maybe having so much to do helped the days go by a little quicker!

Look for God's assignments during the transition times in your life. You may have given up relationships with abusive people you thought cared about you. You only stayed and tolerated it because you didn't know what else to do. But now you are moving away from them, and you feel like you are adrift with nowhere to go. What is the assignment you have right in front of you that will fill your life until you land where God intends you to be?

You might notice that you have a sense of purpose when you help others, as Noah did while caring for his family and the animals. Who needs your attention and care? I am convinced we don't really know how important we are to those closest to us. When our world has been turned upside down, we have to get our thinking right side up again. That means riding out the storm and looking around for others who may be struggling as well.

I imagine that, after tending to those in his care, Noah knew more about animals when he left the ark than when he entered! (An interesting aside: I have noted in my counseling practice that the children who have been abused and adults who were abused as children often have a special love for animals! When people are harmed and have learned others are not trustworthy, pets and animals become an ongoing source of love and comfort.)

I have one last note concerning Noah's escape and God's protection and provision: Scripture never reveals Noah's thoughts or questions before he laid his first plank. He may have wondered, "Why does God allow this brutality? Why doesn't he stop these monstrous people and their horrible atrocities?" We can only imagine that Noah's dread of those people and his trust in God moved him to do whatever God told him to do, with no questions asked.

If God told you to move away from the dangerous people in your life when they refused to change, would you? Are you ready to risk leaving behind all that is familiar? Then step aboard! The ride may get rough. But there is a rainbow, a promise, and a whole new world ahead!

Moses

Whether or not you ever watched the classic movie *Ten Commandments* starring Charlton Heston or the Disney animated film *The Prince of Egypt*, you have probably heard about the life of Moses, a central figure in the Old Testament. He is known as the law giver and the deliverer who led his people to freedom in the book of Exodus. His people, the Israelites, were slaves in Egypt. When their numbers grew, the pharaoh became afraid of rebellion. So he ordered the Israelite baby boys be destroyed (Ex. 1:9–22). Moses' mother coated a basket with pitch to waterproof it. She wrapped her little three-month-old baby in blankets and placed him in the tiny ark. Then she cast him adrift on the Nile River into God's care (Ex. 2:1–4).

The pharaoh's daughter found the basket floating among the reeds. She took him up into her arms, and from that moment on, he became her son and a prince of Egypt. Moses' biological Hebrew mother nursed him, but the Egyptians educated him, and he was raised in the palace (Ex. 2:5–10). When he became a man, however, he noticed more and more of the injustices against his people. And at one point in his life, he went down into the mud pits to work alongside them (Heb. 11:24–25).

One day Moses saw an Egyptian beating one of the Hebrew slaves. Moses killed the bully and tried to secretly bury the body in the sand. The next day, he witnessed two Hebrew men fighting. He asked the one in the wrong, "Why are you hitting your fellow Hebrew?" The man asked, "Who made you judge over us? Are you thinking of killing me as you killed the Egyptian?"

Discovering that his deed was now public knowledge, he left Egypt for the safety of the desert. He knew the pharaoh's wrath and ran to escape from what surely would have been a death sentence (Ex. 2:11–15).

Lots of role changes took place for Moses through the years. He went as an infant from a poor Hebrew family to the luxurious, palatial corridors and royal chambers of the pharaoh's palace. Then as a young man, he left the comforts of the Egyptian life to voluntarily build bricks in the mud pits with his brethren. After that, he found himself in exile, living in the rocky desert.

While Moses was in the desert, he began a new life. He married, had two sons, tended to his flocks of goats and sheep, and lived in tents. Of all the changes in his life, up to that moment, it might have been the years during his wilderness time that he learned patience and humility.

Then one day, while tending his father-in-law's sheep at the foot of Mt. Horeb (possibly also known as Mt. Sinai), the mountain of God (Ex. 3:1), he noticed something on the edge of a cliff that sparked his curiosity. He climbed up the side of the mountain and found there a bush that appeared to be on fire, yet not charred or destroyed. He stared at the blazing sight.

Suddenly the voice of God spoke from out of the burning bush, "Take off your sandals, Moses, for you are standing on holy ground." The voice told Moses to go back to Egypt in God's name and tell the pharaoh to let his people go (Ex. 3:1–22).

Moses was no longer the over-confident young man who left

Egypt. His response to God that day, was, "I don't speak well. What if they don't listen to me? Who do I tell them has sent me?" Doubt filled him. That might have hindered him, had he not stayed long enough with God on that mountain, to build his confidence in the Almighty. Humility often makes us much more usable in our creator's hand than when we are positive we are right and sure in everything we are doing.

Moses probably experienced an inner struggle at the prospect of returning to Egypt. He grew up watching his people be bullied by the same Egyptians that fed and clothed him. He already made the mistake long ago of trying to avenge a wrong by killing the man that he caught beating his fellow Hebrew. He might have thought his people failed to understand his true intentions. Instead they called him out for the self-righteous deed that it was. He might have felt unappreciated and misunderstood. And once again, imagining what going back might mean, he was scared. Old worries may have brought up new concerns. He may have thought, "How credible could I be to my people, whom I abandoned, and my Egyptian family, whom I betrayed?"

All the years Moses was away, raising a family and putting his life back together, the Israelites still suffered under bondage, praying to God for deliverance. Moses was now being asked—no, told—to go back where he was a hunted man. He would not take matters into his own hands as he had tried before, but instead he put his life into God's hands. The Lord would administer his own justice with his own timing and method until his people and their enemies knew that Jehovah God lived.

When you are being bullied or those you care about are being bullied, there will probably come a time when you will have to confront your attacker. Moses had years to think about what he would say to the pharaoh if he ever returned to Egypt. The waiting and preparing for that conversation might be the hardest. But when God pulls you aside alone, he will also give you the words and courage to use them. Exodus 4:12: "Now go; I will help you speak and teach you what to say." And Hebrews 11:27: "By faith he left Egypt, not fearing the King's anger; he persevered because he saw him who was invisible."

Moses told his father-in-law he wanted to go back to Egypt to see if any of his people were still alive. As soon as Moses determined in his mind that he would help his people, God gave him encouragement. Now the Lord had said to Moses in Midian, "Go back to Egypt, for all the men who wanted to kill you are dead." So he took his wife and sons and traveled back to Egypt (Ex. 4:18–20).

God can bring others alongside you before you have to address your bullies. God promised Moses he could have his brother Aaron as his spokesman since Moses had concerns that he himself would be "slow of speech" (Ex. 4:10–17, 27–28). How strange it must have felt for Moses to return to the halls of the palace where he had played as a boy and walked with other princes and his teachers as a man. When he stepped back into the court of the pharaoh, he was not a prince of Egypt, but the representative of the King of the Hebrews.

A different pharaoh sat on Egypt's throne than the one that Moses ran from forty years earlier. But the pharaoh that Moses confronted, nevertheless, was the same bully, controlling and dominating every aspect of the Hebrews' lives. Moses warned the Egyptian monarch many times over the next days that God would bring plagues on the nation of Egypt until he obeyed God and "let his people go." But the pharaoh refused until the last plague took the life of every firstborn son in Egypt, including those in the royal household. (For a full account of the plagues and the Passover night, see Exodus 4:29–12:30.)

The citizens of Egypt gave their former slaves gold and anything they asked for in their eagerness to see them leave. And the Israelites got their first taste of freedom from oppression in over four hundred years! The Hebrews, their parents, grandparents, and great-grandparents had never lived outside of slavery. What an exciting day that exodus must have been (Ex. 12:31–51).

One of the most frightening times in the life of people surviving years of abuse is the moment that it all stops. This is because they don't know what to expect. Is it just a lull before it gets worse?

When the Hebrews left Goshen and Egypt, while standing at the edge of the Red Sea, they heard the thundering sound of horses' hooves and clatter of Egyptian chariot wheels. They must have looked back and thought, "Things just got worse." The pharaoh and his officials had changed their minds and were ready for revenge and the opportunity to get their victims back in line. They lost their crops and firstborn sons. They were not about to lose their easy income in the form of slaves (Ex. 14:5–9).

Nothing but water in front of the Hebrews and a sea of soldiers on horseback behind them meant there was no escape. Moses knew one thing: God had not brought him that far to leave him stranded on a beach. Many of the people were intimidated by the bullies and by the tight spot in which they found themselves. They begged Moses to give up, afraid they would face a more horrible fate if they kept going forward (Ex. 14:10–12).

Moses didn't even consider going back under the heel of their slave drivers. Israel's leader kept his bullies at a distance and his God close to his heart (Ex. 14:13–18). He looked for the Almighty's answer to the problem. Moses cried out to God. Exodus 14:19–22:

> Then the angel of God, who had been traveling in front of Israel's army withdrew and went behind them. The pillar of cloud also moved from in front and stood behind them, coming between the armies of Egypt and Israel. Throughout the night the cloud brought darkness to the one side and light to the other side; so neither went near the other all night long. Then Moses stretched out his hand over the sea, and all that night the Lord drove the sea back with a strong east wind

and turned it into dry land. And the Israelites
went through the sea on dry ground, with a wall
of water on their right and on their left.

The sound of the rushing wind and crashing waves pulling the
water back all night long must have been frightening. A camp of
sleepless refugees listened and wondered what their fate would be
as dawn broke in the morning. A path slowly appeared between
two massive walls of water. Not only did God keep the enemy back,
he also used that "strong, east wind" to dry and harden the once
muddy ground, so the hordes of defenseless people could travel
to the other shore. Did the teenagers run their fingers along the
inside of the wall of water? Were the people excited, or were they
terrified the waves would pour over them at any moment? What
was it like in that tunnel with walls made of water?

When you feel trapped, it is time to trust God and get creative.
Moses prayed to God and looked for a solution that seemed
impossible. But impossible is God's specialty. He knows who is
coming and what is stopping you. He sees how great your obstacles
are and how overwhelming the enemy appears. Your creator will
create a way of escape, and he will deal with those who pursue you.
Take your eyes off the situation long enough to look up expectantly
to see a miracle you never could have imagined.

We might think that the memory of Moses parting the Red
Sea by the power of the Almighty and the Israelites crossing on
dry land would be indelible in each escapee's mind. If not that,
then wouldn't they forever recall how God moved the waters back
together, crashing over their enemies? They did, in fact, tell each
generation about this incredible rescue by God. But it did not
keep them from becoming ungrateful bullies themselves once the
danger had passed.

Moses led his people to the holy mountain. They camped
at the base of Mt. Sinai. And God told Moses to come up alone
and talk with him (Ex. 19:20–31:18). For forty days and nights,

Moses listened as the Lord gave him the Ten Commandments and detailed instructions on how his children should live. Many of our laws today, protecting life and property, are based on those important commands that the Almighty gave on that mountain, for example, "Thou shalt not steal" and "Thou shalt not kill." The Ten Commandments were written on two tablets. The very finger of God etched them in stone on both sides. The Lord handed the stone tablets to Moses to share with his people in the camp below.

When you open God's Word and get away with the one who wrote the book, wisdom and knowledge will pour out to you, as it did for Moses on Mt. Sinai. Moses learned a lot about the practical application of God's words as well.

God was very specific on how he wanted his people to act. He expected purity, integrity, honesty, and compassion. Moses learned all of this in God's company. If you will commit to taking time alone and away with God for forty days, a few minutes out of your day, and listen with an open heart, he can give guidance and courage that you will need in order to handle the bullies in your life.

Moses thought his bullies were the Egyptian soldiers, washed up, dead on the shore of the Red Sea. But his people down in the camp below God's holy mountain had become idol-worshipping bullies. When Moses disappeared on the top of Mt. Sinai, the Hebrews surrounded Aaron and pressured him into fashioning a calf of gold for them to worship and follow. They had "corrupted themselves" (Ex. 32:1–8) in forty short days. But Moses now knew how to deal with bullies and how to lead the others out of bullying and disobeying the God who rescued them.

As Moses walked down through the rocky crags in the mountain, carrying God's law in his arms, nothing could take away his resolve that, no matter what the opposition, he would follow his creator. God had signed his own name on the heart of Moses. The forty days Moses spent in the presence of God prepared, encouraged, and enabled him to lead and intercede to God on behalf of the Israelites for the next forty years (Ex. 32:7–16).

The people complained, grumbled against Moses, and tried many times to undermine his leadership. But what God gives you from his Word when you are alone, he will use in your life later. Hebrews 10:16: "I will put my laws in their hearts and I will write them on their minds." And Ephesians 2:10: "For we are God's workmanship, created in Christ Jesus to do good works, which God prepared in advance for us to do."

You take more than the Ten Commandments down into your camp of bullies. You take God's plan for your life and the power of the Holy Spirit to give you courage and inspiration when you need it most. God never left Moses, and he will never leave you. The Lord may even have people following your lead as you become bolder and more determined to keep your eyes on him.

JESUS

God helped Noah and Moses take others away from their bullies. But he sent Jesus to meet his! This is known as "the temptations of Christ in the wilderness." It is recorded in Matthew 4:1–11 and Luke 4:1–13 in detail and briefly in Mark 1:12–13.

Jesus is not simply another important figure in Bible history. His cross stands at the center of it all. The Old Testament sacrifices and indeed the laws given to Moses on Mt. Sinai pointed toward the coming of Jesus Christ. He would be the one ultimate sacrifice and the sole individual to keep and fulfill each commandment of the law. The New Testament and the future point back to that crucifixion of two thousand years ago. Many people during that time in history suffered an inhumane and horrible death by hanging on crosses that lined the roads of the Roman Empire. But only one crucified man intentionally died on a cross and then left an empty tomb, rising three days later.

Jesus came to earth and took on our frail humanity, intending to die in our place for our sins and open heaven for us. He would be the bridge between his Heavenly Father and his earthly people. But the most cunning bully of all would try to tempt Jesus to worship him and leave us behind.

Let's look at the context for the temptations of Christ. This took place apparently after John baptized Jesus, as recorded in Matthew 3. It was at the beginning of Jesus's ministry. Matthew 4:1–2: "Then Jesus was led by the Spirit into the desert to be tempted by the devil. After forty days and forty nights he was hungry." What an understatement that was!

How weak a starving Jesus must have felt physically, if not emotionally. Forty days and nights without any nourishment had to be torture. Surely Jesus was in the survival mode at this point as Satan moved in to really begin to work on him! Your bullies will look for the times you are alone, weak, and vulnerable. Follow Jesus's example. Jesus always used his wits. He would do that many times over the next three years. And he was good at it!

Like most bullies, the devil began by trying to make Jesus doubt himself. "The tempter came to him and said, "If you are the Son of God …"" If your bullies can make you doubt who you are, then anything is possible. They have the power to hurt you with their words and manipulate you with their suggestions!

Jesus knew himself—who he was and from where he came. But in that forsaken, rocky desert, suffering from horrible hunger and the heat of day and cold of night, he had to also be keenly aware that he was suffering as a human being suffers. Satan was counting on Jesus to use his supernatural powers to help himself instead of obediently relying on his Heavenly Father's plan. Matthew 4:3–4: "'If you are the Son of God, tell these stones to become bread.' Jesus answered, 'It is written: 'Man does not live by bread alone, but on every word that comes from the mouth of God.'"

Jesus knew scripture. He quoted Deuteronomy 8:3. Studying God's Word is not merely an intellectual or emotional exercise. It is for times like these when you feel weak and are tempted to do anything to stop the pain. Bread can disappear in a moment, but the Word of God continues to feed and strengthen you daily for the rest of your life.

The books of Matthew and Luke reverse the order of the next two temptations. They give, however, very similar accounts. Luke records the second temptation as Satan's attempt to get Jesus to follow him and not his Heavenly Father, to be a king without a cross, to rule over us without being the sacrifice for us.

Luke 4:5–7: "The devil led him up to a high place and showed him in an instant all the kingdoms of the world. And he said to him, 'I will give you all their authority and splendor, for it has been given to me, and I can give it to anyone I wish to. So if you worship me, it will all be yours.'"

Bullies desire to have dominance over you. They want you to bow to them and be a type of god in control of your life. They don't want you to think for yourself. But you have the right to choose whom you worship and whom you will follow.

Jesus kept his answer short and to the point. Luke 4:8: "And Jesus answered, 'It is written, 'worship the Lord your God and serve him only.'" You don't have to bow down or serve any bullies, even if they promise you the world. Not only do bullies intimidate and make threats, they make promises they will not keep. When they can't break you, they may try to enlist you as a friend. You have to be wise and know that, if they are bullying you, they are not trustworthy and don't deserve your allegiance. God has a plan for your life. Keep your attention on him.

The third temptation Luke depicts is in Luke 4:9–13:

> The devil led him to Jerusalem and had him stand on the highest point of the temple. "If you are the Son of God," he said, "throw yourself down from here. For it is written: 'He will command his angels concerning you to guard you carefully; they will lift you up in their hands so that you

will not strike your foot against a stone.'" Jesus answered, "It says: 'Do not put the Lord your God to the test.'" When the devil had finished all this tempting, he left him until an opportune time.

Jesus knew all about the verses his enemy quoted. They were from Psalm 91:11–12. But Christ understood the heart of his Father's Word and did not allow the devil to twist it. Satan was pushing Jesus to commit suicide and test his Father's love to see if he would rescue him.

Bullies push kids, teenagers, and even adults to commit suicide. In over twenty years of counseling, I have heard the horrific things people will do and say in order to bully and take control of other people's lives. The news stories and videos on YouTube give accounts of people daring and encouraging others who are struggling with victimization of bullying to end their lives.

One young woman, a teenager at the time, Lizzie Valesquez, came across her picture on the Internet with the caption, "The Ugliest Woman in the World." Lizzie has a rare disorder that keeps her from gaining weight.

She remembers noticing there were four and a half million views and multiple posts demanding she kill herself. She could not understand why people would say these horrible things about her and to her. This was devastating. Fortunately she did not listen to the suggestions that bullies made to her.[1]

Lizzie made it her goal to speak up about bullying and began her own YouTube show. She was invited on many television programs, including the *Today Show* with Katie Couric, to talk about her experience of being bullied. Her TED talk, her own YouTube appearances, as well as a movie made about her life can be seen online. She is now a motivational speaker and an author. (Note: More about Internet and cyberbullying will be covered in chapter 7.) The important point Lizzie continually makes as she addresses bullying is "not to let others define you."

Jesus knew who he was and how much his Heavenly Father loved him when the devil was tempting him in the wilderness. Christ knew the devil tempts us to make us weak, but God tests us to make us strong. Jesus understands what you are going through because he has lived through the pressures you experience now. Don't let bullies define or control you. Refuse to listen when they push you to be self-destructive. Don't believe their promises or be manipulated by their twisted half-truths.

Jesus was strengthened for his ministry by the testing those forty days. He can empower and give you his strength. Luke tells us, which Matthew's gospel does not, that Satan left until an opportune time. Bullies look for opportunities to victimize. But Jesus knows how to deal with those who try to hurt you. And he knows the help you need. Matthew's gospel gives us a fact that is not included in Luke's gospel. Matthew 4:11: "Then the devil left him, and angels came and attended him." Who are your earthly angels in the form of friends or family who would offer encouragement and comfort if they knew what you have been enduring? Give them the opportunity to help!

So what are you going to do between the forty minutes and forty days God has for you to break free from bullies? Noah's forty days in the ark was a time of waiting. But it was also a time of preparing for the journey away from his bullies and toward a new life of hope and promise. Noah invested himself in rescuing his family and the animals God put into his care. What project is God's special assignment into which you can pour your energies while you are pulling away from bullies?

Moses spent forty days on a mountain, taking in God's Word daily, which he would need in order to be the great leader of a nation for the next forty years. What time are you setting aside each day to talk with God and study his Word in his presence? Could he be preparing you for leadership?

Jesus faced off with the worst bully of them all during his forty days in the wilderness. But he gave you a great example of how to deal with those who lie, manipulate, hurt or pressure you to harm yourself. Jesus didn't allow anyone to tell him what his Heavenly Father's plan was. He already had the biggest part in it. Don't let your bullies tell you who you are or who you are not, or what you should do with your life. God already has a unique plan. He is waiting for you to discover it.

Describe a time that you felt like Noah, when it seemed like you were all alone in a world full of bullies.

What was your way of escape?

Who were you able to help along the way?

What do you like best about the life of Moses?

When might have been the scariest time for Moses confronting his bullies?

How did knowing scripture help Jesus combat his bully's lies?

How can you take the same action Jesus did when bullies dare you to take chances with your life?

When has knowing the truth helped you put bullies' lies out of your mind?

What were the lies that bullies told you?

What are the truths you can tell yourself to counter those lies? One example would be:

Lie: You can't do anything right!
Truth: I do lots of things well!

Lie:
Truth:

Lie:
Truth:

Lie:
Truth:

Who are your bullies?

What have you learned in the last forty minutes that could help you break free from bullies over the next forty days?

MY PLAN OF ACTION

CHAPTER 4
Be Bold, Not Timid

Being Bold Is Taking Action Before the Courage Arrives

Freedom lies in being bold.

—Robert Frost

Definition of boldness:
Not hesitating in the face of possible danger
Definition of timidity:
The lack of self-assurance, easily alarmed, shy

—Dictionary.com

If the word "timid" is offensive to you, use the word "unassertive." Take the test below, and determine if you tend to be bold or timid. You may fall somewhere in between the two. This test is designed to raise self-awareness. Use what you learn from the answers to your test and the information in this chapter to give yourself confidence when faced with bullies.

BOLDNESS TEST

Circle the answer below that best describes you:

1.	Is it difficult to tell people no?	A. No	B. Yes
2.	How do you typically deal with conflict?	A. Confront it	B. Avoid it
3.	What is your response when attacked?	A. Defend	B. Ignore it
4.	Would you call yourself "assertive"?	A. Yes	B. No
5.	Are you shy?	A. No	B. Yes
6.	Do you speak your mind or give your opinion?	A. Frequently	B. Sometimes
7.	Do you typically do what you want to do?	A. Yes	B. No
8.	Would you rather others make the decisions?	A. No	B. Yes
9.	Is it easy for you to say what you want?	A. Yes	B. No
10.	Do you like control?	A. Usually	B. Sometimes
11.	Do you try to keep others from getting mad?	A. No	B. Yes
12.	Do you stop people from bullying you?	A. Yes	B. No

SCORING

Add up the answers in column A _____
Add up the answers to column B _____

If more answers fall into the A category, your personality is probably bold. If you have more answers in the B category, you are probably unassertive, or timid. Bullies usually target unassertive or timid people. If you scored high on timid or unassertive points, begin working on changing that score.

How can you become bolder in your life? Pick out at least three of the test questions that you will work on in order to be more assertive. Write out the questions and answers you will change from unassertive (or timid) to bold in the next forty days.

Question # _____

Question # _____

Question # _____

Ideas how I will implement the changes:
(Note: You may want to read this chapter and continue writing in your plan of action section.)

_____
_____
_____
_____
_____
_____
_____
_____
_____
_____
_____
_____
_____
_____

I was doing a book signing at a bookstore one Saturday afternoon. I was talking with lots of people, taking pictures and enjoying the interaction with everyone who came by. Out of the corner of my eye, I noticed what appeared to be a shy little boy of around eleven years old. He was handsome with a slight build that made him appear more to be the age of seven or eight. He had two big green eyes that flashed and then stared downward as soon as anyone looked at him. He seemed very self-conscious as his parents accompanied him to my table.

The boy's mom and dad told me they just happened to be looking for books when they noticed mine. Then they began to share the tragic story of how their happy, carefree son turned depressed and isolated as a result of the last school year. A group of bullies at school had teased, harassed, and tormented their son daily. The parents had talked to the principal several times about the bullying with no success. Finally the little boy's parents had to get him into therapy to deal with the depression.

The saddest part for their son was that he didn't understand why the boys chose to be so cruel to him. The dad told me their son had never been very assertive, but most people liked him right away. The parents had recently taken him out of that school and put him into a smaller, private Christian school where they knew the principal and teachers.

I gave the boy a book and signed it, and then I wished him well. He smiled warmly, opened the cover, and started reading as he walked out the door. I felt sick and sad for that child who bullies had targeted. His lack of assertiveness became a bull's-eye on his back. He was a walking target every day he came to school. When bullies saw that others could push him around, more joined in and made a sport of it.

Some people might score evenly on the test for both boldness and timidity. This could probably be the case for a ten-year-old girl named Michayla. She was friendly and outgoing but withdrawn and passive around kids who were aggressive toward her. She developed a nervous twitch in her eyes, but only when she became nervous or self-conscious. When that happened, the mean kids began to notice her, and she was singled out for bullying.

Robert and Darla were two of those mean kids. Darla was a very pretty girl with long, thick, blonde hair that she wore in a ponytail. She was popular at school. Many of the girls copied the way she dressed and wanted to be like her. Most of the boys had a crush on her. Robert was one of those boys, and he did whatever she wanted, just to get her attention.

Robert and Darla were in the same class at school with Michayla. They rode home on the school bus together. The pair sat in the seat directly behind Michayla each afternoon. They began talking about Michayla's blinking eyes and "how stupid she looked." They talked loud so she would hear and poked her in the back, taunting her, "No one likes you." They lived one block over from Michayla's house, and so they all got off the bus at the same time and place each day on the corner at the end of Michayla's alley. And that was when the bullying got intense.

Every day when the bus let them off and it pulled away, the two bullies began to torment Michayla. One stood in front of her and one in back. She could not go home until they were done pushing her around and calling her names. Michayla liked school and most of the other kids, but she dreaded when the school bell rang at three o'clock and it was time to board the bus for home.

Michayla had admired Darla and how confident, popular, and pretty she was, and she could not understand why the girl she looked up to would want to pick on her. Darla never gave her a reason. Michayla's nervous blinking irritated Darla, and that seemed to be enough to motivate the abuse. Robert wanted to impress Darla, and that seemed to motivate him. Every day when the bus let them off, the two cornered Michayla and threatened her, making it harder and harder for Michayla to get away.

After Darla and Robert got off the bus one afternoon, Michayla, feeling desperate, ran up to the bus driver. She told him what the two were doing to her every day after he dropped them off. The driver followed Michayla off the bus and confronted Michayla's bullies.

"Are you two bullying her?"

"No, we aren't!" they both protested.

The bus driver gave them a stern warning, got back in the driver's seat, and drove away, leaving Michayla alone with two, angry bullies.

"Did you tell him we were bullying you?" Darla demanded.

"No!" Michayla lied, working her way down the alley that led to her backdoor, just five houses away.

Robert stepped out, blocking her path. Michayla was wearing a new, dark navy blue knit hat decorated with bright lemon-colored flowers on it. It was a gift that her mom had bought her that week.

Darla sneered at Michayla and said sarcastically, "I like your hat. It's cute, too cute for you!"

Darla pulled it off her head and threw it over a tall, wooden fence. Michayla was startled and immediately riveted her focus to the spaces between the boards to see her new hat lying in the mud. Michayla quickly turned, crying, and ran home as fast as she could, barely making it to her backyard gate before they could catch her.

When you are passive and finally become bold enough to get help, like Michayla did with the bus driver, things sometimes get worse before they get better. This is when most victims of bullies give in or give up. It is actually the time to keep the momentum moving forward. Keep this in mind: be bolder and braver when you would rather not bother!

What hurt Michayla the most was not the bullying that particular day, but that her mom had given her the new special hat that she loved. Her mother was very careful with money and rarely purchased anything but the necessities. The sentimental value of the gift saddened her the most. She felt a terrible ache in her stomach whenever she thought about it.

That was when Michayla decided to get her mom involved.

She finally told her about the bullying and what happened to her pretty knit hat. She asked her mother to come to the bus stop each day so the bullies would leave her alone. Her mom agreed.

The next afternoon, as the bus pulled away, Darla and Robert backed Michayla up against a cinder block wall in the alley. Michayla's heart felt like it would pound right out of her chest. She looked around. Once again, she was all alone. Michayla could not believe that her mother had let her down. Suddenly Michayla spotted her mom stepping out into the alley, behind her backyard fence, staring at the two bullies. This time Michayla wasn't shy about the fact that she was getting help.

She waved at her mother. "Hi, Mom!" she shouted. And Michayla marched boldly past her two assailants, down the alley to her house.

The bullying stopped after that. Her mom picked her up from school for a couple weeks. Then Michayla began walking home, taking a different route than the bus. She was able to go in through her front door and avoid the alley. She did not ever take the bus again. She never knew if her mom talked to the school or the bullies' parents.

Darla and Robert didn't bother Michayla the rest of the school year. She ignored them on the playground and in the cafeteria. She spent time with her friends. To counter the mean words her bullies told her, she kept saying over to herself one thought, "They lie. I like people, and most people like me back." She gradually gained confidence and began to relax, and the blinking stopped.

There are, of course, worse cases of bullying. She was never physically injured. But the threat of it every day was always there, along with the cutting words, each time they told her she was worthless and that everyone else thought so too. She didn't believe them, and that is what helped her the most and, of course, becoming bold enough to get the help she needed.

If this is happening to you at school, the workplace, or in relationships, tell someone and make a bold move past your bullies just when they are sure they have the upper hand. (I still feel sad about the lovely hat that was a gift from my mom. I never got it back. But I got bolder, and maybe that was more important.) Yes, that was my story.

As a therapist (AKA Michayla), I find it necessary to let my clients know it is not their fault they are being bullied.

Those who have been hurt by others will often ask me, "Is there a sign on my back that says 'kick me'? Is there something wrong with me that others think it is okay to beat up on me?"

Any weakness or slight difference puts a person at risk for becoming vulnerable to bullies. That doesn't mean he or she did anything to cause it. A good example is the elderly lady walking with a cane to the store in a rough part of town.

That frail, female senior citizen does not deserve to be harmed just because she lives where she does. If thieves, however, want money or feel like picking on someone, she will be singled out. Bullies will choose to victimize her over a younger, more able-bodied individual on the same street. Predators want to find someone who will not be a problem. Occasionally we read in the paper about a mugger who is shocked and disabled by the sweet, little old lady, who pulls pepper spray from her handbag and sprays her bully in the face. She may be old, but she proved she is still bold!

You cannot help it if, by nature, you are somewhat passive. However, there are tricks to help you be bold when abusive people confront you. It begins with a mind-set. A determined frame of mind can give you an advantage. Remember, bullies are more likely to push you around if they think they can. You want them to know you may be more trouble than they think. (I wish I had known that as a child!) This does not mean you threaten them. It means you make them think twice before they pick on you. You need a thought or two that keeps you strong.

It will help you to rehearse a few clichés in your mind, little sayings that boost your own morale. Then you will walk around them with more self-confidence. And that looks like boldness to bullies!

Here is one cliché to think about when you are being harassed, "Fake it 'til you make it," which means you act as if something is already true. Act as if you don't care about their opinion of you. Bullies hate to be ignored because it means their words have no power to hurt you. Of course the words sting, but your attackers don't know it. And eventually when you look as if you are bored with the whole thing, you start realizing you really don't care what they think. After all, that is how you "fake it 'til you make it."

Another cliché to keep in mind is, "Don't let them see you sweat." Simply put, that means to keep calm and don't let bullies know they are making you nervous. Here are a few tips: Keep your shoulders back and eyes up, giving everyone else but the bullies' eye contact. Avoid locking eyes with those who are aggressive toward you, as that will appear to be a challenge, unless you are prepared to fight.

But on the other hand, don't ever let your eyes drop to the ground as if you are trying to be invisible. That is a flashing sign saying, "Weak and Helpless." You will become a magnet for anyone wanting to dominate you. Look up. And remember, plans in a bully's mind can't change the resolve in your heart. Psalm 112:8 says, "Their hearts are secure, they will have no fear; in the end they will look in triumph on their foes."

Write down a few clichés you know, or ask friends or family any they have used or heard that might help you when you are under fire. You can record these at the end of this chapter in your plan of action section. Also look through the psalms in the Old Testament when you are in danger. Psalms offer more verses describing God's protection and power than any book in the Bible. Verse after verse will encourage you that God is your refuge and he will help you deal with your adversaries.

King David wrote many of the psalms we find in the Old Testament of the Bible. Much of David's life was spent dealing with bullies. One was sadly close to his heart, his mentor, King Saul. (See *The Book on Bullies: How to Handle Them Without Becoming One of Them.*) If you will write down and memorize one verse a day from Psalms for forty days regarding God's refuge and protection, your boldness will increase daily.

Being timid or unassertive is not a sin! But acting bold can keep bullies at bay. This does not mean you are not afraid or hurt by abusive people, but you refuse to be a victim. Boldness, remember, is taking action before the courage arrives!

How are bullies hurting you with their words? What are they saying? What names are they calling you?

Who are your bullies? Write down their names.

How are bullies hurting you physically? Examples include pushing, hitting, grabbing, kicking, punching, and/or restraining you so you can't move or go places you want to go.

What can you do to be less passive and act bolder when others are bullying you?

How can you make it safe for yourself?

If you are outnumbered or being bullied by someone bigger or more powerful, who can you tell to get someone in your corner to help you? List people who could possibly help.

Remember Mikayla's (my) story. Telling the bus driver didn't help. Telling her (my) mom did. If you tell someone in authority and you still get bullied, are you willing to keep asking other people for help until the bullying stops? Circle your answer below.

Yes   No

When do you usually act passive? What kind of situation is it?

When is it easier for you to be bold?

What cliché or saying are you going to tell yourself each day over the next forty days that will give you confidence and help you be bold? Write it in the space below:

MY PLAN OF ACTION

CHAPTER 5
Recognize Your Personal Strengths

Personal Strengths Are as Unique as Fingerprints

The more you like yourself the less you are like anyone else, which makes you unique.

—Walt Disney

Your fingerprint is special and different, setting you apart from others. Only one set of fingerprints like yours exist. They belong to you! Even identical twins have different fingerprint patterns. The federal government identifies you by your fingerprints. Smart phones and other electronic devices can be opened not simply with a password but with your own fingerprint. God made the tiny lines that circle the intricate pattern on each of your fingers to be especially yours. If he can create a fingerprint to be one-of-a-kind, what else has he created to be unique about you?

God has created you with your own brand of strength. But you have to know what that is and how to use it. Bullies use theirs. You may not feel powerful, but you have power. Knowing your strengths are as important or more significant than knowing your weaknesses when it comes to being bullied. Take the following test to identify your own strengths. Then draw from that knowledge in developing your own formula for handling potentially abusive people.

UNIQUENESS TEST

Circle the answer below that best describes you.

1.	Do you think things will turn out right?	A. Yes	B. No
2.	Do you have a good sense of humor?	A. Yes	B. No
3.	Do you make friends quickly?	A. Yes	B. It's hard for me
4.	Have you kept friendships long term?	A. Yes	B. No–short term
5.	Do you refuse to give up easily?	A. Yes	B. No
6.	Were there hard times you survived?	A. Yes	B. Not really
7.	Do you easily persuade others?	A. Yes	B. Not easily
8.	Are you reasonable and flexible?	A. Yes	B. It depends
9.	Do you like to solve problems?	A. If I can	B. I avoid problems
10.	Do you think you are clever?	A. I can be	B. I'm not sure I am
11.	Are you tough-minded?	A. Sometimes	B. Not usually
12.	Do you set a goal and finish it?	A. Yes usually	B. Not typically

The test you just took addresses six attributes that become your personal strengths. The more answers you marked as A, the higher likelihood that you have resources within you to manage bullies. Which or how many of the six are yours? Write them in the spaces below:

Questions 1–2: Your optimism and sense of humor
Questions 3–4: Your ability to make friends
Questions 5–6: Your resilience
Questions 7–8: Your power of persuasion and ability to work with others
Questions 9–10: Your creativity in problem solving
Questions 11–12: Your mental toughness

Your score: _____

Your strengths: _____

_____

_____

_____

_____

As you think of handling bullies, fighting back may seem like your only option. You see it played out in movies, electronic games, school, and your neighborhood or hear it in stories when people brag about their skirmishes. But the fact is that violence just escalates to the next level or spreads to more people and places. When do you get even? Will you get suspended from school or lose your job for fighting? What keeps you, once the victim, from ultimately becoming the bully, also known as the bully-victim?

The fact is that you will have to handle bullies in a variety of circumstances throughout your life. You need to pull from your God-given strengths that are unique to your personality in order to not be under someone else's control. Let's look at your strengths.

The first category of strengths is your optimism and sense of humor, two qualities that raise you a little above your circumstances. If you are positive or optimistic about life, you see problems as opportunities and believe the best outcome is possible. Therefore, you are not defeated easily. Additionally, if you can find the humor in life and draw others into that point of view, you will lighten the intensity of the moment. A friend of mine who is now a retired principal said he was small in stature as a boy and used his sense of humor to keep some of the bigger boys from picking on him. Many would-be victims use humor to distract and win over bullies. That likability and common ground changes how the bullies view you. It may be temporary, but it can get you out of a tight spot and give you more control. (Note: If your family and friends don't think you are funny, then you probably aren't! If that is your case, then don't try humor on bullies. It will just backfire.)

The second category relates to your ability to make friends. This means you have support when you need it most. (Note: Read more about this in chapter 9.) Friends keep you from feeling isolated, vulnerable, and alone. Bullies like to keep their victims to themselves and get nervous when numbers stack against them. Friends can help to protect you physically, but also mentally and emotionally. Let people know what is happening. That way, the people who care about you can come alongside you.

The third category is your resilience. This is your ability to spring back or rebound from adversity. Very little stress can overwhelm some people. And yet others are like corks that pop back up to the surface even after being held under for an extended time. If you scored on resilience, not only do you survive, you thrive. And you won't be kept down. Make a list of other times in your life that you overcame the odds. If you did it then, you can do it now!

The fourth category is your power of persuasion and your ability to work with others. If you scored in this area, then you have people skills, and you are influential. You probably also communicate well. Don't underestimate yourself. You could have leadership qualities that can turn the tide of events when bullies or bystanders stop to listen to you. You are the type of individual who can reason with others and talk them into seeing things your way. Let go of your fear and concentrate on what you think could sway your adversaries. How have you in the past talked others into doing what you wanted? Sell your bullies on your ideas of how to get along with you and why it is going to be to their benefit!

Your creativity and problem solving is the fifth category. The fact that you chose to read this book, take these tests, and study the devotionals indicates you think outside the box to find solutions. You look for good resources to figure out answers to problems. You are writing down your own ideas as you read or plan new strategies to equip yourself for the next time you are bullied. Because you have problem-solving skills, you can reason your way through emotional situations. You may know you are clever, but not realize that cleverness takes creative thinking. You have both!

The sixth and last category highlights your mental toughness. Your family or friends might call you stubborn. You hang on to a thought or belief like a bulldog. The upside is that you can also be self-motivated, and once you start a project, you want to see it through. You will not simply read this book. You will go out and do what you learn from this text. You decide the right course of action and move on it. You like information, but you have to see the logic or importance of it for yourself. Then you apply it. The caution is this: be stubborn against wrong but softhearted for what is right. Your creator gave you that mental toughness to stand up for the good!

Now that you are aware of your strengths, you know you have resources that are God-given and uniquely yours. Tap into those resources whenever you need them, to break the bully's hold over you. You are stronger than you think you are and smarter than your bullies will ever suspect.

MY PERSONAL INVENTORY

List some of your personal strengths that you discovered in this chapter:

How have you used those strengths in past situations to help you when bullies or abusive people criticized or hurt you in some way?

How can you use those strengths with your bullies today?

Ask friends and family or any supportive people who know you well what strengths they see in you. List those strengths in the space below:

MY PLAN OF ACTION

CHAPTER 6

Empower Yourself; Find and Use Your Voice

If You Don't Speak Up, Who Will?

Wise men speak because they have something to say: fools because they have to say something.
—Plato

What is it about the sound of a voice that elicits such emotion? A mother or father rocking a baby in his or her arms speaks or sings in soft, low tones, helping the child drift off to a peaceful sleep. By contrast, the sound of a loud voice, raised in an angry or sarcastic way with rapid-fire sentences in the same room, can make a baby squirm and cry. The infant doesn't know what is being said. But the air is tension-filled.

Laughter is also a sound that can bring up strong feelings, either positive or negative. Laughter that is warm and engaging is contagious, and you smile even when you don't know the source of the joke or incident. (If you have a bad day and need cheering up, just go to YouTube and look for "laughing babies." Their joy is infectious!)

On the other hand, at the opposite end of the spectrum is the sound of bullies' laughter and jeering. Their type of humor is cruel and malicious, boiling up a variety of feelings within you of anger, hurt, and sometimes shame. Those emotions can influence and darken your thoughts until you hate the abuser and yourself for being abused.

The very sound of a voice singing, speaking, or laughing sets the mood and the atmosphere. On the other hand, language, of course, gives meaning to the words. Words that are used as weapons degrade and injure people. Abusive language that constitutes bullying usually starts a sentence with "You are …" and ends with a demeaning remark. "You are stupid," "You are ugly," "You are ridiculous," and "You don't know how to do anything" become personal attacks. When someone does this to you, the natural response is to come back with a, "Well, you are …," which just keeps the name-calling circling back to the other. Each derogatory name ups the ante, so to speak, for the other person. Nothing gets solved, and tempers get out of control, or resentment gets pushed deep down inside for a later get-even opportunity.

So what do you do to empower yourself when bullies ridicule and tease you? First, remember, if you refuse to give up, the power is still yours. You choose what you believe. You make the decision whose opinion of you matters, theirs or yours. Counter their mean remarks in your head with the truth, "I am smart. I look good, and I do lots of things well!" If you are going to stop the bullies in your life, you have to take control of your own thoughts. Tell yourself the truth and live as if you believe it! Don't allow bullies to dictate their version of you. They don't even know who you are, but you do!

Next, determine how you can use your voice to empower yourself without attacking back. If you are physically hurt or threatened, you would be wise to use your voice to get the help you need for protection. (See chapter 9.) The following questions will help you decide if you have found your voice.

THE VOICE TEST

Evaluate how you empower yourself. Circle the answer below that best describes how you use your voice.

1.	Do you tell others if you disagree with them?	A. Yes	B. Not usually
2.	Have you ever told a bully "Stop"?	A. Yes	B. No
3.	Do you speak up when you have been wronged?	A. Yes	B. Seldom
4.	Do you wait too long to speak up to a bully?	A. No	B. Sometimes
5.	Are you talking to God about your problems?	A. Yes	B. No
6.	Would you tell a close friend if you were bullied?	A. Yes	B. No
7.	Do people listen to you?	A. Yes	B. Not really
8.	If you are taken advantage of, will you protest?	A. Usually	B. No
9.	Do people talk over you or interrupt you?	A. Seldom	B. Often
10.	If you were bullied, did you tell anyone?	A. Yes	B. Not sure

The voice test identifies how easy or difficult it is for you to empower yourself by simply using your voice. Add up your score, and record it in the space provided below.

A. _____

B. _____

If your score is higher in the B column than in the A column, you will need to practice finding and using your voice. Write out three of the questions where you answered B, which you would sincerely like to be able to change to answer A.

Note: Your plan of action at the end of this chapter is an excellent place for you to begin recording how you will change those three answers.

The first individual to whom you may need to start raising your voice is God. You may be thinking, "Susan, you have no idea how long I have begged him for help, and my bullies are still plotting and looking for ways to hurt me! I have given up hope."

That is because "hope" is not a word in your vocabulary! Long ago, you resigned yourself that there was no hope. You know how to live without it. You are afraid you will be disappointed by thinking life will be better, only to watch it crash once again into a million pieces.

My answer to you is this: remember, the secret in the preface of this book, "Your story is not over! The best is ahead, not behind you." Many Bible heroes suffered at the hands of bullies, and it was not their fault either. And life seemed to have come to a standstill for them as well. But they never gave up hope or stopped talking to God.

The Old Testament tells the intriguing story of one great Jewish man, Daniel, a target of several bullies. The backdoor bullies plotted to not only hurt but destroy Daniel. This story can be found, interestingly enough, in Daniel 6.

Daniel was probably a teenager when he and his friends were taken captive and made to serve the king of Babylon. If that were not bad enough, bullies in the new country tried to make life miserable for him and attempted to have him killed. By the time King Darius came to power, Daniel had been in captivity for over sixty-five years and was probably in his eighties. He had been a faithful servant, honest and straightforward with the king's predecessor and King Darius.

During King Darius' reign, Daniel had become a man of influence and vision. The officials, called satraps, and administrators were jealous of the close relationship that had developed between Daniel and the king and Daniel's rise to power. Daniel 6:3–5:

> Now, Daniel so distinguished himself among the administrators and the satraps by his exceptional qualities that the king planned to set him over the whole kingdom. At this the administrators and satraps tried to find grounds for charges against Daniel in his conduct of government affairs, but they were unable to do so. They could find no corruption in him, because he was trustworthy and neither corrupt nor negligent. Finally the men said, "We will never find any basis for charges against this man, Daniel, unless it has something to do with the law of God."

So the bullies set their plot and flattered the king by having him sign an irrevocable decree. The law read that everyone in the land was to worship no other gods but the king himself for thirty days. Even so, Daniel continued to worship the Lord. He knelt, looking toward Jerusalem, his homeland, before an open window, praying aloud three times a day, thanking God and asking him for help. The bullies heard this and confronted the king with his own edict. So a reluctant and distraught king had Daniel thrown into the lion's den.

That had to be the longest night of Daniel's life, as he was dropped into that den of lions, and the giant rock closed off the opening above him. Did the hungry lions pace and circle, stalking him? Did they lunge or reach out and try to swat him with their claws? Were they threatening him with deep, growling sounds in their throats? Maybe they finally fell asleep, leaning their large bodies against him in the dark pit. What we do know is what Daniel called up to the anxious king, who rose at dawn, hoping to find him alive. Daniel 6:21–22: "O king, live forever! My God sent his angel, and he shut the mouths of the lions. They have not hurt me, because I was found innocent in his sight. Nor have I ever done any wrong before you, O king."

Your bullies may have put you, like Daniel, in one of the loneliest, most frightening situations you could have imagined. But wherever you go, God goes with you, even into the lion's den. No matter how terrifying and awful the bullying was in that room, you did come out alive! That room was dark and frightening with those that wanted to devour you; however, the Lord had other plans for your life. You are here now by God's grace.

We can only imagine the prayers that Daniel spoke throughout that endless night. When the king realized God had spared Daniel, he was relieved. Then in a fit of rage, he had Daniel's enemies thrown to the very lions that were intended for him. The king then promoted Daniel to a place of prominence in the kingdom of his captivity. Daniel lived for many years, and the Jews, the king, and the people in his kingdom admired him. The man who survived that long night still had a future, holding a powerful, affluent position that most people would envy. Bullies had a plot, but God had a plan.

Daniel's friends were devoted to God as well. They were taken captive (along with Daniel) by King Nebuchadnezzar and renamed Shadrach, Meshach, and Abednego. These accounts can be found in Daniel 1. The three men faithfully served King Nebuchadnezzar. And they showed integrity and diligence in all the tasks they performed. They had their jealous bullies too.

"Some astrologers came forward and denounced the Jews"

(Dan. 3:8). The bullies pointed out to the king that the three Jews did not bow to the ninety-foot, golden image the king had built and decreed all should worship. The bullies reminded the ruler that their punishment was death in a fiery furnace (Dan. 3:9–12). The king confronted the Hebrews about the accusations. But the Jews would not back down.

They simply stated their position, "If we are thrown into the blazing furnace, the God we serve is able to save us from it, and he will rescue us from your hand O king, But even if he does not, we want you to know, O king, that we will not serve your gods or worship the image of gold you have set up" (Dan. 3:16–18). The furious king ordered the furnace to be stoked until the heat was seven times hotter. The guards assigned to take the men to their destination got too close to the furnace and died from the heat (Dan. 3:19–23).

The king watched. Would the roaring fire cremate the Jews? Then God showed up! When the king looked into the blazing furnace, he saw four, not three, figures. What kind of conversation went on between the friends and God in the heart of the fire that day? Perhaps they simply stood quietly in God's presence, amazed. The king recognized that the Lord was there in the flames. And when they came out of the furnace, the three Jews did not even smell of smoke. Their clothes, hair, and bodies were not the least bit singed. (Dan. 3:24–27).

Having the courage to speak up for what you believe when you are being pressured to withdraw your stand is difficult. But even more intimidating is the threat of physical harm if you insist on not backing down. Gangs, like those astrologers, are sure you won't have a will or a way out of your predicament.

God blessed the faithful three. He gave them favor with the king from that day forward. The king then decreed across the land that anyone who criticized the God of those three men would be punished. (Dan. 3:28–30).

Bullies do not have the last word on your life. Each of those

Bible heroes mentioned above kept their relationship with God intact. They used their voices to talk about God and to God. They spoke up for their Lord and their faith, putting their lives at risk. God did not forget them. But they had to hang on to their creator and pray to him in faith while he worked on their behalf. God cares about your difficulties, and you have his ear.

Psalm 142:6 says, "Listen to my cry, for I am in desperate need; rescue me from those who pursue me, for they are too strong for me." The psalmist who wrote this knew how to use his voice and didn't hold back anything. He didn't try to be eloquent or edit himself. He believed, as he poured out an honest prayer in a private audience with his creator, that he would be heard!

Paul shared the importance of voicing specific needs to God so he could pour peace into broken hearts until the answer comes. Philippians 4:6–7: "Do not be anxious about anything, but in everything, by prayer and petition, with thanksgiving, present your requests to God. And the peace of God, which transcends all understanding, will guard your hearts and minds in Christ Jesus."

The above verses are evidence that God wants to hear from you and he can change you in your circumstances, equipping you to handle the tough stuff. This begins by replacing fear with a petition (request) to God and thanking him ahead of time for an answer you have not yet seen. Pray, knowing God's understanding of your situation is transcendent or far surpassing any mere human insight.

When you lift your eyes and fix them on God, he promises he will change the way you see the problem. Like a guardian standing watch, God will protect, so your mind, where you reason, and your heart, where you resolve, are steadfast in Christ Jesus. "But in everything present your requests to God." In other words, keep talking to him.

The next individuals you need to address are your bullies. Most bullies push people around because they can. Peer groups are reluctant to tell them it is wrong. Bullies go through life running over people with their behavior and their words.

How can you speak up to bullies who have controlled you with fear over a long period of time when they show no intention of stopping? Is there any hope that a bad situation will ever change? Let's look at a time when the world watched that happen!

The years after World War II, during a period known as the Cold War, the communist government of the German Democratic Republic (GDR), East Germany, the puppet state controlled by the Soviet Union, began to build a barbed wire and concrete wall that would hold East Germans captive for nearly three decades. On August 13, 1961, the wall was constructed. The huge barricade consisted of a block wall, a space, and another fence with a minefield between them. The area between the wall and the fence was called the "death strip," as many people died there trying to escape to West Germany. The wall in the capitol city was known as the Berlin Wall.

The wall went through the middle of neighborhoods, with one side of the street being in East Germany and the other in free West Germany! If you looked on a world globe back then, you would have seen two countries called Germany. Families were torn apart, and their relatives were separated for years. Disney made a compelling movie, *Night Crossing*, a true story of a family in East (communist) Germany who risked their lives to build a hot air balloon and escape over the wall, floating to freedom in the middle of the night.[1] A more recent movie, *Bridge of Spies*, directed by Stephen Spielberg and starring Tom Hanks, shows a little of life behind the Iron Curtain.[2]

My husband and I lived in Germany when it was divided. He was a sergeant in the army, stationed on a US Army base in the little town of Fulda in February 1969. We lived in a house across a meadow from the base. My husband was on border patrol and travelled the miles of fence. By then, the Soviet Union had constructed tall fences in the countryside where we lived. The tall barbed wire fence was the demarcation of what was known as the "border," again with a death strip of mines between the two fences.

Many times I heard the sirens from my house, putting us all on alert. Usually that meant the Russian and East German armies could be approaching the border in their tanks, and ours prepared to meet theirs to keep them from crossing over into West Germany. Czechoslovakia had just been invaded by the Soviet Union, leading Warsaw Pact troops, on August 20, 1968, just six months before our arrival. The United States and free West Germans were on constant alert that the Russians would invade West Germany next. My neighbors lived daily under this horrible threat for years, and East Germans lived with the reality of it.

One day President Reagan was visiting West Germany and made a speech that has since gone down in history. He stood before the Berlin Wall on June 12, 1987, at the Brandenburg Gate, and in front of the whole world, he raised his voice, demanding, "Mr. Gorbachev, tear down this wall!"[3]

God knew what many did not that, behind the scenes, Gorbachev's Soviet Union was running out of money and keeping their troops in East Germany was no longer possible. They could not afford to pay them, and the East German government was crumbling. In the meantime, the citizens in that communist country were becoming bolder and began to feel empowered. They were taking their case to the streets and using their voices to speak out against their bullies. The people and even some police were chanting together, "We are the people."[4]

Two years after President Reagan's speech, November 9, 1989, the GDR announced the border would be open for travel for Easterners to West Germany. East German men, women, children, and teenagers walked and then swarmed through the checkpoints, breaking down gates and climbing over the infamous wall for the first time in twenty-eight years as their uniformed bullies stood by with loaded guns, afraid to shoot.[5] Then the citizens of East and West Germany danced on the wall and tore it apart together.

God may be weakening your bullies' position while you are getting bold enough to use your voice and change the course of events in your life. I often wondered if the East German people heard the voice of President Reagan's inspiring speech. The East German soldiers could not quiet his voice or the words that came from the microphone, filling the air and drifting over the wall.

President Reagan spoke boldly and raised his voice in opposition against those who had controlled so many people's lives over the years. He called out the one person (Gorbachev) who was, at that time, responsible for the oppression. Ronald Reagan announced on an international stage what he expected to happen. Meanwhile the citizens of East Germany were raising their voices to their bullies.

When bullies' position of power gets weaker, and you get stronger, as God works for you behind the scenes, a new day of freedom dawns! Some evidence for this comes from Fredrick Taylor, an expert historian on Germany, who provides in his book *The Berlin Wall* insight into what was happening weeks before freedom day.

> Despite veiled threats and savage action against individual protestors, during the annual 40th anniversary weekend, 70,000 of Leipzig's citizens flocked to the next Monday prayer meeting at the Nikolaikirche (kirche, translated, means church), which had **become** the most important single focus for opposition.[6]

Two days after the Berlin Wall fell, the West German newspaper headlines read, "Wir Danken Alle Gott." Translated, it means, "We Thank God."[7]

So now it is your turn to stop the bullies in your life. You will have to raise your voice in protest if you want the bullying to stop. How can you communicate exactly what you want but were afraid to say?

First of all, if you are going to confront your bullies, keep it simple. "Stop" is the shortest sentence with the biggest impact. Say "Stop!" like you mean it. Don't give an ultimatum you can't deliver. By not answering their reply, "What are you going to do about it?" you keep them wondering. Though I heard of one boy who answered his bully, "You won't like it!" Both tactics give you time to think of a course of action. Look a bully in the eye. This is a time of confrontation.

If you think there is a misunderstanding, then you will want to get that handled before a confrontation starts. Asking a few questions could open a dialogue and help you find out why bullies are picking on you. They may think you bullied them first or said something malicious about them at school or work. By asking or saying, "Why are you saying that?" "Did I do something to you that I don't know about?" or "I don't know what the problem is, so why don't you tell me?" they may tell you what their rationale is for being mad or irritated with you. That does not make it true or give them the right to bully you. But it could give you information you didn't have and the opportunity to set the record straight. Some bullies may then stop if they are bullying in retaliation for a wrong they thought you had done to them.

What if you ask and bullies tell you about a threat, gossip, or slander that you actually realize did originate with you? All you can do is tell them you are sorry and will try to set that straight. Don't expect them to appreciate your honesty. They will be angrier because you just confirmed what they only suspected.

The good part about a conversation with your bullies is that you also get the chance to correct exaggerations and distortions that often go along with gossip. So be sure to ask exactly and specifically what they heard you allegedly said about them before confessing to anything! You want to know what has been embellished or added to the story. Once they've told you everything and who told them, correct the errors, and give them a reason or context for your conversation about them. Keep your explanation short! Get to the point, give them the situation, and correct any distortions.

Communication is the only way to clear up misunderstandings. No one can read your mind, so if you want others to know what you think, tell them. Using your voice is proof to your bullies that you won't suffer in silence any more. After all, if you don't speak up, who will?

MY PERSONAL INVENTORY

What would you like to say to those who keep bullying you?

Write out exactly how you want to say it:

What questions do you have for your bullies?

Write out exactly how you would like to ask those questions:

Circle one or more answers below:

Next time my bullies attack me, I am going to say, "Stop!"

Yes   No   I will try   I will if the time is right

I am going to speak up to bullies or others who can help me!

Yes   No   Maybe

MY PLAN OF ACTION

CHAPTER 7
Avoid Traps

Don't Play in Minefields/Cyberbullying

Be more concerned with your character than your reputation, because your character is what you really are, while your reputation is merely what others think of you.

—John Wooden

CYBERSPACE SAFETY TEST

Circle the answer that is more generally true of you:

1.	Have you ever shared your password?	A. Never	B. Once maybe more
2.	Are social media/privacy settings on?	A. Absolutely	B. Not sure
3.	Have you said mean things on devices?	A. No	B. Sometimes
4.	Do you text with people who hurt you?	A. No	B. I have at times
5.	Did you group text gossip online?	A. No	B. To be included
6.	If you keep getting mean texts, you …	A. Block	B. Read them all
7.	Will you tell if you are cyberbullied?	A. Yes	B. Keep it to myself
8.	Do you think you are texting TMI?	A. Never	B. If I feel safe
9.	You text or post when you are angry.	A. Try not to	B. To defend myself
10.	You are off electronics and your phone	A. Frequently	B. Almost never

Add up your score and record it in the space below:
Scoring: A. _____ B. _____

If you scored more answers in the B column than in the A column, you may become a target for cyberbullies. After reading this chapter, journal in your plan of action ideas you read here or those you think could boost your score in the As. But remember, even if you try to take precautions, no one can be sure he or she is immune from cyberbullying.

Just because you were singled out or attacked by cyberbullies, that does not mean you did anything wrong or you deserved the abuse. However, being proactive and protecting yourself as well as reporting the bullies or the bullying can make it stop and keep you from being caught in the cyberbullies' trap.

Have you ever felt like you were stepping into the bullies' trap? You didn't realize it, but suddenly there it was in front of you. This can feel like you are walking around in a minefield, never quite sure when or where the danger will be. All around the world, teams of experts try to find and disarm or explode real mines that were hidden during wartime. The technicians look for the most likely places for hidden explosives. Some have maps of where the bombs were hidden. They have to be very aware, careful, and observant so they don't get hurt or killed in the process.

The writers of Psalms and Proverbs had a firsthand knowledge of what it was like to be caught in the bullies' trap. These insights and prayers resonate with anyone who has felt hemmed in by bullies.

Highlight or underline the prayers or verses about traps that have the most meaning for you.

- Psalm 31:4—"Keep me free from the trap that is set for me, for you are my refuge."
- Psalm 38:12—"Those who want to kill me set their traps, those who would harm me talk of my ruin; all day long they scheme and lie."
- Psalm 141:9—"Keep me safe from the traps set by evildoers, from the snares they have laid for me."
- Proverbs 11:6—"The righteousness of the upright delivers them, but the unfaithful are trapped by evil desires."
- Proverbs 12:13—"Evildoers are trapped by their sinful talk, and so the innocent escape trouble."
- Proverbs 28:10—"Who ever leads the upright along an evil path will fall into their own trap, but the blameless will receive a good inheritance."

What are hidden traps that bullies use to hurt others? Cyberbullying has become one of the more recent mine fields. 25 percent of all teenagers have experienced this type of bullying, according to a study done by Justin Patchin and his colleagues at the University of Wisconsin-Eau Claire, surveying 15,000 middle school and high school students across the United States.[1] Girls are somewhat more likely to bully via electronics than boys.[2] That may be because they are more verbal. But both boys and girls are involved with this type of silent bullying.

Cyberbullying is one of the most devastating types of bullying to the people who are being injured by it. It is done on computers, tablets, smart phones, online games where they can also chat while playing, and social media, to name a few. The targeted are impacted because of the cyberbullies' long reach, making their bullying and those being bullied visible to a large, gullible audience. Until recently, victims of cyberbullying didn't have much recourse for setting the record straight or getting misinformation or unwanted photos off the Internet.

If you are being cyberbullied, you are not powerless. Unfortunately many news reports over the last decade have been about kids who felt powerless and overwhelmed, to the point that they resorted to committing suicide, while never telling anyone they were victims of cyberbullies. Cyberbullying can be lethal.

If you have been thinking about suicide, tell someone, and remember that suicide is a permanent solution to a temporary problem. You know, if you spend any time on the Internet, that information and pictures come and go every second and are replaced by newer ones in the next moment. But that is no comfort if you have been targeted and wonder who all is looking at what has been posted about you. There are ways you can take back your power, stop your cyberbullies, do damage control, and make the bullies accountable.

If you are a student and you have been cyberbullied, these are some strategic moves you can make now! If you read or see something on the Internet about you, specifically anything inappropriate or of concern to you, or sent to your email or text, do the following:

1. Tell your parents. You will need support, and they may want to talk to authorities. Explain to your mom and dad you don't want to lose your phone and electronic privileges! (Unfortunately that fear keeps students from letting their families know how they are being victimized! On the other hand, your parents may restrict computer or

electronic use or confiscate your phone for a short period of time so they can monitor and collect information vital in building a record of offenses that can be given to district attorneys or the police.)

2. Don't answer the bullies back.
3. Always print out and save cyberbullying messages. It can be used against them as evidence, as can voice mail recordings and handwritten notes.
4. Have a parent go with you to talk to your school principal.
5. Change your screen name, and give it only to people you trust.
6. If threats are made, have your parents call the police and the Internet service provider.

If the cyberbullying violates the law in the form of harassment, threats, or stalking, then your bullies just crossed over into criminal territory and can be punished for their actions. If cyberbullying involves sexually exploitive pictures or sexting, bullies may have to register as sex offenders.[3]

Another point to remember is that, though the cyberbullies think they can attack anonymously, the police and the Department of Justice are getting better at tracing posts back to computers, tablets, and cell phones.

Here are a few tips to keep you out of trouble in the future from cyber-bullies:

1. Never give your password to anyone, even a friend. If you did, change it!
2. Avoid sending impulsive and angry messages (flames).
3. Stop texting in capital letters, as it may be misunderstood as yelling.
4. If something about you is posted to a website, tell law enforcement, as officials can subpoena records of all web users for a particular website.

5. Stay off of bash boards (online bulletin boards where people post who or what they hate, usually used to bully someone).[4]
6. Don't participate in happy slapping, where a victim is bullied and an accomplice stands by, making a video on the phone to post later online. If you are the victim, try to identify the accomplice as well as the attacker. Both may be guilty of bullying.[5]
7. Turn off your phone and get your number or email address changed if you are a target of text wars (a group sending hundreds of emails and texts, flooding your phone as a form of bullying).[6]
8. Contact your social media site if someone opens a new account under your name. That is a form of "impersonation."
9. If threats are made, have your parents call the police and the Internet service provider. From there, users can be tracked to their individual computers, tablets, or cell phones.

Here are some resources if you are ever cyberbullied:

- http://wiredsafety.org, a website that provides assistance
- http://www.cyberbullying.ca-a, website for students, parents, and the public that describes the emotional costs of cyberbullying, forms of mistreatment, and prevention strategies

If you are an adult and you are cyberbullied by coworkers on the job, you have a variety of actions you can take. Office computers and all emails are the property of the agency where you work. Print out a copy of all toxic or denigrating messages you receive. Do not respond, but save these copies until you are ready to show your supervisor, employer, or human resources department.

If the coworkers are texting you the harassing remarks to your cell phone, send it to your home computer. Email and print hard copies that will also show the phone number of the recipient. Then block the cyberbullies' telephone numbers. Take these hard copies to your employer, supervisor, or human resources department. As a last resort, change your cell phone number and tell your coworkers who are your friends to not give it to other coworkers, even if they ask for it.

As in the case with kids, if a text or email is a threat, harassment can be seen as a case of stalking. Then it is criminal. You have the choice whether you want to pursue legal action or not.

What do you do if your bullies are attacking your business by posting awful reviews on your website that are untrue, with the intent of ruining your reputation? Marketing consultants will probably advise you to hire them to help clean this up on your website. And you may need to do that. But you can also address the critical comments in one of two ways. Make your apologies to the critics on your public webpage, and request they try your product, service, or business one more time. Let them and anyone reading the complaint and your response to the complaint know you strive for excellence and customer service. People read your reply, and they can quickly realize if that person gave an honest critique or if you are being bullied.

Another way to take the offense toward bullying on your website is to thank people for their reviews and assure them you care about improving, which hopefully you do. You can also ask (in person) other satisfied customers to please post reviews of your service and products.

Most businesses want to know how they are doing and rely on reviews occasionally to give them feedback. But reviews that rant and rave, filling up the web page, are probably bullying you.

For example, someone posted a terribly critical review that went on and on about the pastry at one of my favorite bakeries. The reviewer took a picture of a pastry that looked like a semi truck had run it over. I knew it was something I had never eaten for breakfast at that bakery shop! I wondered if this critic were actually a competitor. The bakery didn't even know the review was on their website until I told them. I gave them my name and told them I would be glad to give a good review to counter it.

Being constructively criticized to help you develop and grow is nothing like being bullied. Remember, bullying is more of a character assassination. It is meant to hurt, not help, and it is done in a mean spirit with ill intent. The power imbalance is obvious when the attacks come as anonymous cyberbullying.

The good news is, when you know how to stay out of those traps and minefields, you can enjoy technology and all it has to offer in business, education, entertainment, and social networking. What most of us forget is that we can turn all of our technology off whenever we want. You can't help it if cyberbullies get into your cyberworld, but you don't have to let them continually get into your head. Know when to turn it all off, and let it go.

MY PERSONAL INVENTORY

Have you ever been hurt by cyberbullies? If so, what happened?

How did you deal with them and the cyberbullying?

What are you doing or whom are you telling so it will stop?

After reading this chapter, what are you planning on doing to protect yourself from cyberbullies?

How are you helping others who have been victims of cyberbullies?

MY PLAN OF ACTION

_____
_____
_____
_____
_____
_____
_____
_____
_____
_____
_____
_____
_____
_____
_____
_____
_____
_____
_____
_____
_____
_____
_____
_____
_____
_____
_____
_____
_____

CHAPTER 8

Keep Your Distance

Hold On to Your Boundaries

A healthy relational boundary is the imaginary line that gives us both the space we need.

Boundary Test

Circle the answer below that comes the closest to describing you:

1. You put up with abuse if you need that relationship. A. Seldom B. Often
2. You let yourself be bullied so you aren't left out.   A. Never   B. Possibly
3. You tolerate being bullied to keep from being alone. A. No   B. Sometimes
4. You feel a strong need to be liked by most everyone. A. No   B. Yes
5. You want to keep the relationship with your bullies. A. False   B. True
6. If you set a boundary, bullying will just get worse. A. Not true B. True
7. Negative consequences result in setting boundaries.   A. Maybe   B. Usually
8. If you remove the bullies' control over you, you will … A. Be happy B. Lose
9. You worry more when your bullies are not around.   A. No   B. Yes
10. It isn't the right time to distance your bullies.   A. Not true B. True

Add up your score in the A list: _____

Add up your score in the B list: _____

    If more answers are in category B than in category A, you will need to work on setting healthier boundaries with those who bully you. That may mean putting distance between you and your bullies. After reading this chapter, write your answers from the B list and what you are learning and what you want to change. Record your thoughts in your plan of action section at the end of the chapter.

    The definition of "boundary," as used here, is a limit. It is an imaginary line. So if you are setting boundaries on your bullies, you are deciding how much distance you will put between you and them. This distance might be physical space or time apart. The limitation may be their access to you.

    This chapter addresses the need for distance between you and your bullies and why you may have trouble achieving that. As you took the test, you may have noticed that the focus changes halfway though the questions. The first five questions address the fear of alienation and the fear of isolation as possible reasons why you have not yet put distance between you and those who abuse you. The second group of questions—six through ten—deals with the fear of retaliation. It never quite feels safe to tell bullies "no."

Throughout my years doing therapy, I have worked with certain individuals who have had a hard time putting distance between themselves and those who perpetually bully them. They stick with others who are caustic out of fear that, if they don't, they will be alienated from their peer group or face social isolation. "If I don't go with them, then I will be the one left out and talked about when they get together," that is, fear of alienation. "I don't like how they treat me, but they are my friends, and if I leave, I won't have anyone. I'll be alone," that is, fear of isolation.

Another reason people stay in abusive relationships or don't move away from bullies, even if no real relationship exists, is the fear of retaliation. "I need this job, but everyone here gives me his or her work to do. They are in their own clique. They laugh about what they can get me to do for them. They have been here longer, and if I complain, they will work it around so that I am the one that gets fired," that is, fear of retaliation.

Fear keeps kids and adults from moving away from bullies or setting a boundary with them. The "what ifs," which mentally predict the worst scenario that could possibly happen, keeps people paralyzed and scared. I am often told in my office, "I try to imagine the worst so I am prepared when it happens."

But I tell my clients that imagining the worst that could happen is not preparation. That is rumination and obsessive worry, which takes away hope and the ability to make rational decisions. If you are doing this, it will drain away your energy and pull you down into depression and a feeling of helplessness. You will become very anxious. Then you are less prepared for the future!

Rachelle dreaded 12:00 every afternoon because it meant lunch with the other girls at the office. They would ignore her, talk over her, and belittle her by criticizing her remarks whenever she ventured an opinion. She began to wonder if she wouldn't be better off bringing lunch and eating at her desk or running errands until lunch hour was finished. But she knew, if she didn't go, they would talk about her, like they did the other women in her department. The lunch bunch didn't just stick a fork in their salads but into every absentee who, they imagined, had given them any trouble that day.

Rachelle's friends or coworkers were backdoor bullies. You may have encountered these at some time. They act like friends, and so you let them into your life, only to find they are underhanded in the way they treat you while in your presence and in your absence.

Why did Rachelle keep going out with these women? Probably she put up with their company out of fear of retaliation. She knew anyone who didn't go with them got verbally roasted by the bullies. She didn't want to be one of those victims. But what Rachelle failed to realize was that she was already a victim by being criticized, ignored, and subjected to hearing mean remarks about people she liked. If this is happening to you, confront the group by disagreeing with their criticisms of you and your absent friends. If they continue, let them know you won't be going to lunch anymore or simply stop going. That then becomes a boundary. It is as if you were saying, "If the gossip goes, I stay. If the gossip stays, I go."

Rachelle's first inclination to eat at her desk or run errands on her lunch hour would probably have made her feel a lot better at the end of the day. She could have asked someone else to lunch or gone out with a friend who wasn't in her work setting. Fear of alienation kept her from putting the distance she needed between herself and her bullies.

Sixteen-year-old Joe was the new guy at school. He learned how to handle bullies and potential bullies at an early age. His family moved often because of his father's job. Each time his dad got a transfer, Joe got a new school and another year of being the outsider. He tried to join in with the other students on campus, but they all had their own friends by the time he arrived in the middle of the year. They didn't seem to want a new guy in their group. His social life at the different schools varied. Some students were friendly, but often he felt like he didn't fit in, as he had little history with the other kids. Sometimes he was ignored or bullied.

Joe had learned to be friendly to everyone but not to push too hard for acceptance. He knew from past experiences that not everyone was going to accept him right away. Most of the time he was okay with that. As he made acquaintance friendships, it helped him feel more included. He managed to be on the fringe of several groups, though he didn't eat lunch with the same people each day. He would find one person in each group who liked him rather than try to win them over all at the same time.

Joe's new acquaintance friend in each group, usually but not always, became his connection to the others. Joe's strategy—or social survival skills—kept him from being worried about social isolation and alienation. If someone else at the lunch table began to bully him, he simply said, "Goodbye! See ya later!" and left. He had learned how to set up a boundary and the usefulness of a little distance.

One day, a gang at Joe's new high school began taking over the hallways. They moved as a group, slowly and methodically intimidating students they met. The leader of the group, with his gang beside and behind him, approached Joe as he was walking to class. He began challenging Joe and calling him names. The kids behind Joe stopped to see what would happen, not wanting the gang of bullies to shift attention to them!

Joe recognized a familiar face in the gang. His name was Juan. They had a class together and had shared jokes and games in the cafeteria. Joe ignored the lead bully as if he had not even heard him.

"Hey, Juan." Joe nodded at his friend and smiled as he moved through the crowd and walked into class.

Joe put distance between him and the lead bully and set a boundary by moving away and ignoring him. Because Joe had an ally in Juan (see chapter 11), Joe was less concerned with the immediate retaliation from the bullies.

Life in high school was complicated for Joe because he was continually trying to find his place in a new community and make friends. He had some good times and some tough times. But he learned a lot about himself. He learned not to let the fear of alienation, isolation, or retaliation keep him from setting healthy boundaries. That included new friends who were nice to him and excluded students when they tried to bully him.

Some bullies make the threat of retaliation very real. If you try to pull away, these bullies threaten to take things away from you. They make it difficult for you to have relationships with other people you care about, hurt your reputation, or abuse you verbally or physically.

Unfortunately some bullies may be counterfeit friends, relationships you have at school, or coworkers. These may be your backdoor bullies. If you have tried to talk to them about their behavior toward you and reasoned with them and they continue to do it, distancing yourself may be an option. The time apart may be an opportunity for them to reconsider how they treat you. But whether they change or not, you have taken away their power over you.

After reading most of this chapter, you may still be anxious, imagining that bullies might pay you back for distancing yourself. Toxic people use this threat to stop you from getting away, knowing, if you are afraid what they might do, you won't do anything. Clients who come to me for relief and advice express this very fear, which keeps them controlled by their bullies. "He or she hurts me, but it is not as bad as it used to be. If I try to get away, he or she has ways to punish me that are worse than what I am going through now."

If you are tolerating bullying out of fear of retaliation, you are giving bullies full control of your future. The threat it will be worse if you pull free is a lie. That lie is like an anchor attached to a heavy chain of fear that entangles you, dropping you into a deeper and deeper ocean of despair. Pull yourself loose, come up for air, and start swimming away as fast as you can!

Putting distance between you and bullies is not going to make the situation worse. You may be afraid of all the "what ifs" running through your mind. You are running ahead to what could happen. Right now tell yourself the truth of today, not the fear of tomorrow. It won't be worse later. It has been and is worse now!

Hold on to your boundaries. They are helpful and can save you. A warning sign in front of a cliff is a boundary that keeps you from falling over the edge. A crosswalk is just paint on pavement. But that one-dimensional boundary helps provide a safer way to the other side of the street. A fence around a bullpen tells you there is nothing to fear as long as you keep your distance and stay outside that boundary. How are you going to set your boundaries with bullies and use time or distance when you need it the most?

Why is it difficult sometimes to set healthy boundaries with people?

When bullies push in on you, how are you going to hold your boundaries?

When were you able to put a little distance between you and your bullies? How did you do it, and what were the circumstances?

Have you tried to stay in relationship with bullies out of fear of isolation, alienation, or retaliation? Circle one:

Yes   No

If you answered yes, circle any of the reasons that apply to you:

Fear of isolation   Fear of alienation   Fear of retaliation

Explain your answer:

Find a verse in Psalms where the psalmist felt threatened by bullies. Write it here. Did he believe God would protect him? Sometimes he was discouraged and simply prayed for help. Other times he talks about God being his help. Find the verse that best describes how you feel.

Write out the names of the bullies from whom you need distance. Then write whether the distance you need is a matter of time, space, or both:

What are some ways you can get distance of time or space with those who are bullying you?

MY PLAN OF ACTION

CHAPTER 9
Forgive Bullies; Don't Trust Bullies

Forgiveness Is a Gift; Trust Must Be Earned

Love all, trust a few, and do wrong to none.
—William Shakespeare

The first question that comes to your mind after reading the title of this chapter may be, "Why do I have to forgive bullies when they have made my life so miserable?" The second question might go something like this, "How do I forgive and be able to trust that bullies won't keep bullying me?" The answer to both those questions can be found in scripture. Then the secret power to actually forgive will come from the Holy Spirit, who inspired the writing in the first place.

Why do you need to forgive? Before the question is answered, be sure you understand what forgiveness is and what it is not. Forgiveness is not overlooking, minimizing, or excusing a horrible injustice or hurt that was done to you. Forgiveness is the act of relinquishing anger and resentment toward someone for an offense he or she has done to you. In other words, you are not excusing the behavior, but forgiving the person.

So the first question still needs to be answered, "Why is it necessary for you to forgive bullies?" The number-one reason is that God forgives you for all the wrongs you have done to him and others. Put a checkmark by any of the following verses that are meaningful to you, and write them on your plan of action at the end of this chapter.

- Psalm 130:4—"But, with you (God), there is forgiveness."
- Daniel 9:9—"The Lord our God is merciful and forgiving."
- Psalm 86:5—"You, Lord, are forgiving and good."
- Matthew 6:14–15—"For if you forgive other people when they sin against you, your Heavenly Father will also forgive you. But if you do not forgive others their sins, your Heavenly Father will not forgive your sins."
- Matthew 6:12—"And, (Lord), Forgive our debts as we forgive our debtors."
- Psalm 130:3–4—"If you, Lord, kept a record of our sins, who could stand? But with you there is forgiveness, so we can, with reverence, serve you."

- Mark 11:25—"And when you stand, praying, if you hold anything against anyone, forgive them, so that your Father in heaven may forgive your sins."
- Psalm 103:3—"(God) Who forgives all our sins and heals all our diseases."
- Matthew 5:43–44—"You have heard it was said to love your neighbor but hate your enemy, but I tell you to love your enemies and pray for those who persecute you, that you may be children of your Father who is in heaven."
- Luke 23:34 (during Christ's crucifixion, he called to his heavenly Father from the cross)—"Father, forgive them, for they do not know what they are doing."
- 2 Corinthians 2:10–11—"Anyone you forgive, I will also forgive and what I have forgiven in the sight of Christ, for your sake in order that Satan might not outwit us; for we are not unaware of his schemes."

The number-two reason to forgive your bullies is so you don't inadvertently become a bully yourself, also known as a "bully-victim," in your quest for revenge. Remember, the majority of school shooters (though certainly not all) were once victims of bullying. They retaliated against their tormentors and, many times, the innocent who were merely bystanders.

Anger is a God-given emotion that serves you well so you are not passive when wrong is done. It supplies you with adrenalin to defend yourself or someone else. Just as all emotions have a purpose, like happiness or sadness, so anger has its place. It is energy that moves you to action when danger is present. But anger that has no relief will do damage. Forgiveness is relief, not just for the recipient of your anger, but for you.

Anger is not a sin. Scripture supports this. Psalm 4:4: "In your anger, do not sin; when you are on your beds, search your hearts and be silent." The psalmist is encouraging some soul searching when you feel angry.

The danger with lack of forgiveness is that anger will fuel itself and become a seething bitterness that eats at you or an uncontrollable rage that acts out, hurting you or others. Both of these outcomes sabotage your life and make you a captive to your hatred, locking you up in your own self-made prison. Mentally despising anyone and ruminating about injustices will poison your personality. What you spend the most time thinking about influences what you might ultimately become. Proverbs 27:19: "As water reflects a face, so a man's heart reflects the man."

The apostle Paul writes some interesting comments addressing the number-three reason to forgive enemies. Romans 12:18–21:

> If it is possible, as far as it depends on you, live at peace with everyone. Do not take revenge my dear friends, but leave room for God's wrath, for it is written: "It is mine to avenge, I will repay," says the Lord. On the contrary: "If your enemy is hungry, feed him: if he is thirsty, give him something to drink. In doing this, you will heap burning coals on his head." Do not be overcome by evil, but overcome evil with good.

The passages in the book of Romans give two sides of the same coin. The coin could be seen as forgiveness. One side is the Christian repaying bullies with kindness, feeding them or giving thirsty enemies a drink. The other side of the coin is the wrath of God, which can make your bullies so uncomfortable that they are sorry for what they have done and repent and can then have God's forgiveness. But whether the bullies repent or not, these verses tell you to let God be God.

So now that you have three solid reasons why you need to forgive, how do you forgive? Forgiveness is much easier once you realize it is not the same as trust. Christ asked his Heavenly Father to forgive those crucifying him, yet he never trusted himself into the hands of the Pharisees who put him on that cross. He was very careful to not get caught in their traps. Until the time chosen by his Heavenly Father for him to go as a sacrifice for the sin of the world to the cross, he never let his enemies bully or capture him.

You can forgive people who have been unkind to you, but that does not mean you need to trust them. Putting yourself back into a dangerous situation is unwise and needs to be considered carefully. Once you have talked with your bullies and enlisted support around you for safety, then you can decide if you want to try a relationship. But be wise.

Jesus understood the balance between being loving without being carelessly trusting. He sent his disciples out, two by two, to evangelize and share the good news, or gospel. But he warned his disciples, "I am sending you out as sheep among wolves. Therefore, be as shrewd as snakes and as innocent as doves" (Matt. 10:16). That statement seems strange until you look closer at his meaning.

Jesus wanted his disciples to be as gentle and peaceful as doves. Think of that type of bird that anyone could hold cupped in his or her hand, without fear. Most people would not feel threatened by a gentle dove. But Jesus also painted a contrasting word picture when he told them to be wise as serpents.

Snakes are not easily stepped upon, as they know how to get out of the way quickly and how to hold their own against a predator. They are clever and careful. And they are always aware of their environment and their surroundings. The admonition Jesus gave to his disciples could be his word to you today: Be innocent. Be kind. But also be wise.

THE FORGIVENESS / TRUST TEST

Circle the answer that is generally true of you:

1. You stay mad when someone hurts you.   A. Not for long   B. Yes
2. You don't get mad; you get even.   A. Not really   B. I try to

3. Can you easily let go of past hurts?	A. Usually	B. No
4. Do you forgive people quickly?	A. Most of the time	B. Rarely
5. Do you plot revenge in your mind?	A. Not typically	B. Sometimes
6. Can you see another's point of view?	A. I try to	B. That's hard
7. Do you hold grudges?	A. Not usually	B. Often I do
8. Are you a little too trusting with people?	A. I am careful	B. Probably
9. Are you in harm's way because you trusted?	A. No	B. I might be
10. Do you keep going back even if you get hurt?	A. No	B. Yes
11. Do you trust people you don't know well?	A. No	B. Yes
12. Have you trusted dangerous people?	A. No	B. Probably
13. Do your friends say you are gullible?	A. No	B. Yes

SCORING

Add answers from questions 1–7 in column A: _____

Add answers from questions 1–7 in column B: _____

Add answers from questions 8–13 in column A: _____

Add answers from questions 8–13 in column B: _____

WHAT THESE RESULTS MAY MEAN

If you have more answers from questions 1–7 in column B than in column A, you struggle with forgiving people, and that may include yourself. Find verses in the Bible, or use the ones given in this chapter to shift your perspective and help you move to a place of forgiveness. Write these down in your plan of action section at the end of this chapter.

If you have more answers from questions 8–13 in column B than in column A, you are trusting those who have not necessarily shown themselves to be trustworthy. This does not mean you need to be paranoid or suspicious of people, but it may highlight for you where you need to be more aware and cautious. You don't have to put yourself in harm's way by getting back into abusive relationships, to prove you have forgiven them. Forgiveness may or may not be something bullies ever know you have given them. It is a gift from God that he pours into your heart, and you pass it onto them many times without them knowing or caring.

One of the most amazing true stories of forgiveness comes from the accounts of Corrie Ten Boom. I heard her tell the following story. She, along with her sister Betsy and their elderly father, hid Jews from the Nazis inside their Dutch home during WWII. They were eventually caught and thrown into the same concentration camp as their Jewish friends. Corrie watched God do many miracles in the prison camp, and one was not letting the Nazi guards see a little Bible she wore around her neck on a string. She and her sweet sister Betsy conducted Bible studies with the other female prisoners, undetected. But along with the miracles also came the cruelty of the guards on a daily basis and the starvation, which finally took her sister Betsy's life.

After the war, Corrie attended church one Sunday, when out of the doorway stepped one of her former guards that she remembered well from her dark days in the concentration camp. He was dressed in civilian clothes, smiling and talking with the other parishioners. No one but Corrie knew who and what he was.

Corrie stood paralyzed with rage. Then the awful moment came when he stood in front of her and stuck out his hand for her to shake. Her memory of that Sunday was how frozen she felt until, as she described it, "The love of Christ took hold of me and came down my arm and into my hand." She faced her monstrous bully and shook his hand. She could only do this by the power of the Holy Spirit and the overreaching of God's love. The man did not even recognize or care about the woman he had bullied, though she stood there, forgiving him.

Shaking her abuser's hand was a perfect example of some very difficult passages. The little Dutch lady demonstrated the principles of forgiveness Jesus spoke about in Luke 6:27–28, "But I tell you who hear me: Love your enemies, do good to those who hate you, bless those who curse you, pray for those who mistreat you."

Corrie became one of the most sought-after speakers and evangelists in postwar history. She wrote forty-six books, including

The Hiding Place and *In My Father's House*. Had she let anger turn to hatred, the gift of forgiveness she offered outside the church that day would never have been hers.

Forgiveness is a gift that blesses the giver far more than the receiver. The former Nazi did not know that she had forgiven him and may not have even wanted it. But Corrie was God's child, and she would never have been able to speak with authority to others of the grandeur of God's love and how to forgive unless she had experienced it fully herself.

God has an incredible life ahead of you. Corrie, I am pretty sure, never could have envisioned how her heavenly Father would use her on such a wide scale after the war. It was not her experiences in the concentration camp that empowered her to help people. It was her experience with God before, during, and after the camp that gave her something to offer others.

You don't ever have to shake a bully's hand! You don't need to trust your bullies to be able to forgive them. Forgiveness may be instantaneous or a very long, lifetime process. But let God's power to forgive quiet your angry turmoil until you one day are free to forgive others as God has forgiven you.

Why do you think forgiving bullies is so hard to do?

This is a good place to put down your anger on paper. List all the things they have done to you and how it hurt you.

What is the difference between forgiveness and trust?

How would forgiving those who have hurt and bullied you free you from carrying the anger and hatred around each day?

What do you get out of forgiving someone who has wronged you?

Why does God want you to forgive your bullies according to some of the scriptures listed in this chapter or other verses you have read?

What is the difference between forgiving your bullies and trusting your bullies?

Why would you forgive bullies and still not trust them?

Are there ever situations when you can forgive and trust bullies?

Explain what the following statements mean to you:
Forgiveness is a gift:
Trust is earned:

MY PLAN OF ACTION

_____
_____
_____
_____
_____
_____
_____
_____
_____
_____
_____
_____
_____
_____
_____
_____
_____
_____
_____
_____
_____
_____
_____
_____
_____
_____
_____
_____
_____
_____
_____
_____
_____

CHAPTER 10
Refuse to Be Intimidated

Big Is an Attitude!

Attitude is a little thing that makes a big difference.
—Winston Churchill

The heavy iron door slammed behind us with a clanging sound that echoed down the hall. "Ten free people coming through," the guard shouted as we moved down the corridor. Then we left the safety of the main building and stepped out into the vast men's prison yard with the towering fences.

The prison outreach was one of my favorite ministries. My husband, seven other friends from our church, and I followed our minister and an unarmed correctional officer through the men's medium-security prison yard one winter night. We were going to the little chapel in the middle of the yard to worship with the inmate believers and any of the other convicts who found their way there.

Nothing could have prepared me for how I would feel walking through a sea of men in the prison yard. And nothing could have prepared me for the experience of worshipping with the Christian congregation of convicts once we entered the little church. As Pastor Bill led the singing and our friend John played the piano, the men stood and lifted their hymnals high up in the air. I recall the loose threads hanging from the bindings of the faded, red hymnbooks in their hands.

I heard the old hymn "Blessed Assurance" booming from men's voices with enthusiasm and determination. Their faces seemed to literally shine with a joy I have rarely noticed in any church I have ever attended. They were claiming each promise in every verse, "Blessed assurance, Jesus is mine, oh what a foretaste of heaven divine." Their voices reached the rafters! Their faith was contagious! Suddenly the words meant more to me, and the music was brighter and more hopeful than any time I have sung it, before or since. Then we all sat down.

I will have to admit here, though Pastor Bill's sermon was compelling and inspirational (one of his most dynamic sermons), that night I nevertheless had trouble paying attention. I am embarrassed to say the mountain of muscles, particularly biceps on one of the men in a short-sleeved shirt in front of us, distracted me. He leaned back and rested both of his arms over the back of the pews. He was doing a better job than I, listening intently to what Pastor Bill was sharing.

I looked over at my husband, who smiled, nodded toward the pew in front of us, and whispered to me, "His arms are bigger than my thighs." It seems we were both pretty impressed.

After the sermon, different men stood and asked for prayer, not for themselves, but for their Christian brothers who were being bullied and persecuted for their faith.

The stories were alarming. Their bullies were threatening their lives. But there was a tenderness in the men's voices as they shared, "Pray for brother Jake, for his safety, and for him to be bold and not intimidated as he shares Christ with the other men. He's been threatened, but he has a good attitude. He is standing strong."

One man after another asked for prayer, not so much for himself, but for brothers in Christ who were being bullied and by other prisoners. Then we heard whispering among the men in the back of the sanctuary and noise coming from outside the chapel. Our correctional officer went to the phone on a table and began looking back at us, answering, "Yes, we will."

Then he turned to the congregation but looked directly at our little group and addressed us all, "There is a riot in the medium-security yard, and no one will be able to leave the sanctuary."

I must have had a concerned look on my face because the man with the bulging biceps turned and began to reassure me, "Please don't worry. No one will harm any of you. We will protect you if anything happens."

Whatever the problem in the yard, in a little while it was handled. No explanation was given, and we never asked what happened. We were able to leave within the hour. As we said our goodbyes, the Christian congregational members kept expressing their appreciation that we had come to worship with them. They were especially grateful to Pastor Bill. They turned to each other and patted their Christian brothers on the back, the prisoners and the free men. The Christian convicts gently shook hands with the women in our group as they thanked us over and over again.

We walked back through the medium-security yard into the main building where we had first entered the prison. The iron door closed behind us again as a correctional officer announced, "Ten free people coming through."

I was a little sad for our new friends who could not leave with us. Yet I was sure many of those same men had hurt and victimized others or been bullies at one time. God, however, was transforming many of their lives and others through them as they stood up for their faith and one another. Their attitude and resolve helped them stand against bullies they lived with every single day in prison.

Bullying does not have to be life-threatening to be frightening. You may not be in prison, but you may feel that way when it is happening to you. The Christian convicts had a positive attitude about what God could and would do. And their bullies were not going anywhere soon!

Attitude is a way of feeling or thinking about someone or something that you settle into until it is eventually reflected in your behavior. You know people who have a positive attitude most of the time. They are optimists. They are confident and will take on problems, believing they can work out solutions.

Being bullied can take away all of your optimism and confidence. You may doubt whether you can do anything after being berated and continually criticized by your attackers. The important part that attitude plays in warding off the effects of bullying is in knowing that you have a future greater than the obstacles that bullies pose.

Many famous individuals who went on to do great things in their lives were treated badly by their own bullies. Here are just a few well known people who were bullied, having had some bad memories but bright futures. This list can be found on the Internet under the following heading, "Famous People Who Were Bullied as Kids: 13 Celebs You'd Never Guess Were Bullied As Kids." (Here are ten listed below.)

- Lady Gaga was teased for wearing wild costumes, which now, along with her singing talent, have made her famous.
- Sandra Bullock traveled with her mother to Europe, and when she came back, she wore different clothes than the other kids and was called a "clown."
- Rihanna was criticized for her light complexion and green eyes.
- Tyra Banks, the famous supermodel, was called an "ugly duckling" in her childhood by the other kids in the neighborhood.
- Robert Pattinson of *Twilight* fame was beaten up for his love of acting.
- Jennifer Lawrence was bullied at school. Her quick wit saw her through rough times. She believes it is easiest to ignore negativity.
- Jackie Chan, known for his world-famous martial arts, was bullied as a child for being "too scared."
- Jessica Alba was bullied so badly that her dad had to accompany her into school each day to avoid being attacked.
- Michael Phelps, the Olympic swimming champion who achieved twenty-three gold, three silver, and two bronze individual medals, more than any other Olympian has done to date in history, was bullied in school about his ears, a lisp, and long arms, (the very appendages that pulled him through the water, putting him in the world record books).
- Prince Harry was called "ginger" by other kids because he had red hair.[1]

Bullies can terrorize you and make you doubt yourself. Focusing on your future is hard when you are just trying to get through the day without being accosted. To keep from being disheartened, you need to know that your mind set and attitude will make all the difference. Lou Holtz, the ninth most winning coach in college football history, has noted, "Ability is what you're capable of doing, motivation determines what you do but attitude determines how well you do it."[2]

What can you do in forty minutes to forty days to boost your own confidence and change the outcome when you are being bullied? Take the short test below and find your fearlessness!

THE FEARLESS TEST

Circle the answer that best describes you:

1.	Were you ever brave in a scary situation?	A. Yes	B. Never
2.	Can you make good decisions for yourself?	A. I have	B. Not usually
3.	Have you ever stood against peer pressure?	A. Yes	B. Rarely
4.	Have you come to someone else's rescue?	A. Yes	B. No
5.	Can you imagine standing up to a bully?	A. Yes	B. No

SCORING

Add up all the answers in column A: _____
Add up all the answers in column B: _____

SCORING RESULTS

If you have more answers in column A, you have the ability right now to stand up to bullies or deal with them directly or indirectly. That may mean talking to them, confronting them, reporting them to those in authority, or deciding on a plan to protect yourself. You are able to decide on strategies that best fit your situation, based possibly on what you have already learned from this book.

If you have more answers in column B than in column A, you lack confidence, which does not mean you lack courage! You need to start remembering who you are and accurately retrieve information from your past accomplishments. What you have been able to do before, you can do again. Your fear of failure or getting hurt or bullied worse in the future keeps you from standing up to your bullies today.

Use your plan of action at the end of the chapter to journal about each answer. Write down positive examples from your life. These are samples of what could translate into fearlessness for the difficulty you face today. Those examples are your record and will shore you up when bullies try to intimidate you. If you have trouble recalling situations when you showed fearlessness, ask family members or friends that know you well and have history with you to relay incidences they remember.

Now that you see you have inner resources and there is fearlessness in you that you didn't know you possessed, the bullies need to see it too. That is much harder, especially if you are smaller. So keep in mind the title of this chapter, "Refuse to Be Intimidated." Remember the subtitle, "Big Is an Attitude."

Michael Jordan, the famous basketball player, believed in the importance of a positive attitude, "My attitude is that, if you push me towards something that you think is a weakness, then I will turn that perceived weakness into a strength."[3] You don't, however, need to be as tall as Michael Jordon to be confident and accomplished. Napoleon Bonaparte, born in 1769, was the emperor of France and is still considered one of history's great commanders, yet he was only five feet tall. He was teased in his youth because of his height. His nickname was "Little Corporal."[4]

You can make a big impression without being big! Many famous celebrities and accomplished actors are much shorter in real life than they appear on the big screen: Robert Downey Jr., Ryan Seacrest, Jack Black, Michael J. Fox, Josh Hutcherson, Dustin Hoffman, and Zac Efron[5] are just a few.

Yul Brynner was only five-foot-eight in height and played the king of Siam in the Broadway musical *The King & I* and won an

Academy Award for his part in the movie. He was the king on the stage for many years. He was short in stature, but his bigger-than-life persona filled up the stage. Mr. Brynner stood tall and proud. He sounded and looked six feet tall. He spoke with authority, and you believed those couple of hours watching him perform that he was *the* king.

Tom Cruise is five-foot-seven (and was bullied as a child), but as you watch him on the big screen, you don't doubt that he can hold onto the cliff of a mountain or the outside door of a jet in midair with only his fingertips in one of the *Mission Impossible* movies. Celebrities who are big box office draws look and act the part. They are believable.[6]

If you are going to face off with your bullies or manage them until you can stop them, you have to act the part of someone who refuses to be intimidated. And you have to be believable. But first you have to believe in yourself! Breaking free means breaking with an old belief system that says bullies are more powerful, bigger, stronger, and in control of you.

Remember the first definition of bullying in chapter 1? Bullying is when others are aggressive and repeat their aggressive acts with a power imbalance in their favor. When you believe you have greatness and act on that, you are changing the power imbalance.

Stand tall, and put your shoulders back. Look up and out and never down when around bullies, as stated in earlier chapters. This needs to be reiterated here. Remember those few Christian convicts in the chapel and their confidence, that they could protect us from whatever threat would come through the door. Their refusal to be intimidated gave us courage. You have a presence and poise that demands respect. If you believe it, others will believe it too. "Big sometimes is an attitude." You are on *Mission Impossible*, but with God, all things are possible (Mark 10:27).

Do you remember a time in your life when you had to have courage to help a person or maybe even an animal in trouble?

Why do you think fear of danger didn't keep you from helping them?

What are you afraid could happen if you stand up to your bullies or get help in standing up to them? What has happened in the past?

What could you do to lessen the danger to yourself and still stop the bullies?

Do you remember a time bullies tried scare tactics and you were not very intimidated by them? Why?

How can you keep from being intimidated without becoming a bully yourself?

MY PLAN OF ACTION

CHAPTER 11

Enlist Help and Support

There Is Safety in Numbers

Alone we can do so little; together we can do much.

—Helen Keller

ENLISTING SUPPORT TEST

Take the test below and circle the answer that best describes you and what you believe:

1. I would never tell someone if I were bullied.   A. False   B. True
2. I always handle my own problems myself.   A. I get help   B. I don't like help
3. Asking for help is not a sign of weakness.   A. True   B. False
4. I will get in more trouble if I report bullying.   A. False   B. True
5. I would rather keep problems to myself.   A. Sometimes B. Usually
6. Others can help me if I am bullied.   A. True   B. False
7. I have no one to talk to about problems.   A. False   B. True
8. Others are interested in my problems.   A. True   B. False
9. I should not have to ask for help.   A. False   B. True
10. Together we have power to change things.   A. True   B. False

Add up the answers in column A: _____
Add up the answers in column B: _____

If you have more answers in column A, you probably are more apt to enlist help and support when you are in trouble or are being bullied. You trust others care about you. You believe people will do something to come to your aid or defense once you let them know what is happening.

If you have more answers in column B, you may have trouble asking for help. Your trust level is low, and you can be a little cynical at times. You will need to write these out in your plan of action and examine why you think you are the only one who can handle difficult situations, like bullying. You may have been disappointed or hurt by people who you thought were in your corner, and so you only depend on yourself.

Letting people be a part of the solution can resolve many problems like bullying. This was the case for a young woman named Esther, who saved her people from one of the deadliest bullies in Old Testament history. Esther 1–10 could possibly be considered the most riveting book in the Bible. You won't read about chariots and soldiers in hot pursuit. There's no sound of swords crashing against one another in great battles or spectacular miracles, like the parting of the Red Sea. But if you start reading the accounts and history of Esther, you may not want to put it down until the story ends! It reads like a novel with a plot that takes surprising twists and turns.

The heroine of the book was a young Jewish woman known as Hadassah but also called Esther. She never expected to confront a bully or save her people. Like most who encounter bullies, she was just minding her own business, not trying to attract their attention.

This chapter is all about enlisting help and support. But Esther could not have been more alone. She was from a community of Jewish friends living in captivity in Persia in the house of her cousin Mordecai, who raised her as his own daughter. The king's soldiers abruptly took her away to join the Persian king's harem. Esther had no rights and no way of escape. She kept her nationality a secret on the advice of her adopted father, Mordecai. And she kept her wits about her!

Esther's story really began with King XerXes, the king of Persia. One evening, he held a lavish banquet for his nobles and governors and demanded in his drunken state that Queen Vashti come and put herself on display for his guests. To the king's shock and embarrassment, she refused. So the king had her exiled.

King XerXes then began scouring the kingdom for a young maiden to be the new queen. Esther came upon the scene. After evaluating all of the girls brought to him, she was his favorite, above all the rest. He crowned her Queen Esther of Persia.

Next on the scene came Mordecai, her adopted father. He stayed close by the palace gate so he could inquire about Esther's welfare. One day he overheard a plot by two palace guards, planning the assassination of the king. Mordecai sent a message to warn Esther. So the plot was averted, the guards were killed, and Mordecai's good deed was recorded in the king's record book.

The villain in this true story was the wicked Haman, a ruthless, narcissistic bully and the right-hand man to the king. Xerxes had decreed that everyone bow and honor Haman. Each day, as Haman rode by on his horse through the streets of the city, people bowed to him. However, Mordecai, being a devout Jew who neither worshiped idols nor man, stood tall, never lowering his head. He refused to bow even after the Jewish men in his neighborhood warned him, out of concern, for the possible consequences. Haman began noticing Mordecai and resented him. Anger turned to revenge, and he hatched a plot to kill Mordecai and destroy all of Mordecai's people, the Jews.

Haman convinced the king that the Jews were not loyal subjects, that they disobeyed the king's commands and could not be trusted. The king told him to do what he wanted with the Jews. King Xerxes handed over his signet ring to Haman.

The king did not know that Haman was going to use his ring as an irrevocable stamp on an edict, for the extermination of all Jews in the land. Haman became the Adolf Hitler of his time. Without so much as a hesitation, the narcissistic bully began targeting one man and extended his cruelty to an entire people.

But it would seem that God was working behind events, though his name is not mentioned in the entire book of Esther. Now when Mordecai heard of the edict for their extermination, he stood in the gate in sackcloth and ashes, a sign of mourning and death. When Queen Esther heard about this, she sent a messenger with clean clothes for her cousin. But he refused and sent a message back, informing her of the horrible edict, and begged her to go and talk to the king on their behalf.

Queen Esther reminded her cousin that she could be killed if she approached the king without being summoned first. Mordecai advised her, "If you remain silent at this time, relief and deliverance for the Jews will arise from another place, but you and your father's house will perish. And who knows but that you have come to your royal position for such a time as this?" (Est. 4:14).

Has anyone ever felt more trapped by bullies? Esther's husband had been tricked into becoming her bully by one of the most notorious bullies, Haman. If she approached her husband, the king, to give him that information, she could have been executed immediately. If she did nothing, her people would have been murdered and perhaps even herself once the king knew she was also a Jew. What a lonely, frightening place to be. She had a crown but no power and no friends in power to rescue her.

Esther refused to be a victim. She enlisted help everywhere she could find it. This began with prayer to God. Though prayer is not mentioned, fasting is. And prayer is strongly implied and was traditionally done along with fasting by Jews when seeking God's help in a crisis. But she did not do this alone. She responded to Mordecai's warnings with a plan that required help from others, "Go, gather together all the Jews who are in Susa, and fast for me. Do not eat or drink for three days, night or day. My attendants and I will fast as you do. When this is done, I will go to the king, even though it is against the law. And if I perish, I perish" (Est. 4:16).

Esther put on her royal robes and stood at the inner court where the king could see her from his throne. He saw her and "was pleased with her." And he raised the scepter to her, asking what she wanted of him, "to half my kingdom, it will be given to you" (Est. 5:3). Queen Esther was wiser than her years and used an amazing amount of self-control not to blurt out her problems right then and there.

Esther apparently understood the importance of timing. She may have wanted to make sure she was in the king's good graces and that her bully Haman was off his guard before making her appeal. She asked the king to come for a private banquet she had prepared and to bring Haman.

The king happily agreed. He and Haman dined with Esther that night. After the king had drunk some wine, he asked her again what she wanted, "to half of my kingdom and it will be given to you" (Est. 5:6). Esther simply asked that she be permitted to play hostess to another banquet for he and Haman with the promise she would disclose her request at that dinner. The king agreed.

Elated, Haman went home after the dinner, bragging to his wife and friends that he was the only one invited to the banquet and private audience with the royal couple. Haman's excitement was dampened when he noticed Mordecai sitting once again by the king's gate. He complained to his wife and friends. They suggested he have a gallows built for Mordecai and ask the king the next morning for the Jew to be hung from it. Haman was thrilled with that idea. The gallows were built.

God, it seems, had even better timing than Esther. For that night, the king could not sleep, so he began to read heroic accounts of valor written in the royal record book. He came upon the heroism of Mordecai and how he saved the king's life.

The next day, the king was contemplating how he could reward Mordecai. He asked who was in the court, and someone replied, "Haman." So the king had Haman summoned.

King Xerxes asked Haman for his counsel, "What shall be done for the man, in whom the King delights to honor?" (Est. 6:6). The egotistical, narcissistic Haman imagined the king referred to him. So Haman declared the man should wear one of the king's robes, ride on the king's horse with the royal crest, and be paraded through the city. And it should be announced, as he rode through the streets, the king's pleasure with this individual. To Haman's horror, King Xerxes exclaimed, "Go at once. Get the robe and the horse and do just as you have suggested for Mordecai, the Jew, who sits at the king's gate. Do not neglect anything you have recommended" (Est. 6:10).

Imagine Haman's horror and humiliation. He led the king's horse through the streets of Susa with Mordecai riding, dressed in the king's robes. And all throughout the day, Haman announced the praises of Mordecai!

Haman was beside himself with frustration and seething with hatred. Probably his one consolation was his upcoming private invitation to the second banquet Queen Esther planned for the king and Haman that evening. Haman left for the banquet, probably feeling smug that at least he was still the most important man in Persia, next only to the king. After all, no one else again was asked to attend this dinner with the king and his queen!

The private feast lasted for two days. Most likely the festivities consisted of eating, drinking, laughter, music, and talking. But more was going on behind the scenes. For Esther was setting the stage for the moment she would enlist the help from the one person who could help her the most, her husband, who had unknowingly become her adversary by his total disregard for the lives of her people.

Enlisting help and support may not be easy, but it is necessary. You may have a situation where you are sure, by telling someone in authority about bullying, you could be the one punished. That was the risk that Esther took that night because the alternative was to stand by and let her bully dominate. She was not going to let that happen. She waited for the right time and used her voice, boldness, and all her strength to spring the trap and expose her predator, Haman.

The second night of the second banquet, after the king had drunk some wine again, he asked about her request. She carefully worded her petition.

> So, Queen Esther answered the King, "If I have found favor with you, O King, and if it pleases your majesty, grant my life-this is my petition. And spare my people-this is my request. For my people and I have been sold for destruction and slaughter and annihilation." King Xerxes asked queen Esther, "Who is the man who has dared to do such a thing?" Esther said, "The adversary and enemy is this vile Haman." Then Haman was terrified before the king and queen. The king

got up in a rage, left his wine and went out into the palace garden. But Haman, realizing that the king had, already, decided his fate, stayed behind to beg Queen Esther for his life. Just as the king returned from the palace garden to the banquet hall, Haman was falling on the couch where Esther was reclining. The king exclaimed, "Will he even molest the queen while she is with me in the house?" As soon as the word left the king's mouth, they covered Haman's face. Then Harbona, one of the eunuchs attending the king said, "A gallows seventy feet high stands by Haman's house. He had it made for Mordecai, who spoke up to help the king." The king said, "Hang him on it!" So they hanged Haman on the gallows he had prepared for Mordecai. Then the King's fury subsided (Est. 7:3–10).

The story did not end here. But the bully's plot did. The king could not rescind his edict to kill the Jews, as Haman had used the king's signet ring to seal the orders. That made the declaration legal and binding. Nothing could stop it.

So the king sent a second declaration, allowing all Jews in his country to be able to defend themselves, if attacked. Because of the second order, the Jews disposed of many of their enemies. Queen Esther's cousin and adopted father, Mordecai, was then made the king's chief advisor. "Mordecai, the Jew, was second in rank to King Xerxes, preeminent among the Jews, and held in high esteem by his fellow Jews, because he worked for the good of his people and spoke up for the welfare of all the Jews" (Est. 10:3).

Esther and Mordecai were foreigners, living captive in a foreign land. But they lived a life of integrity in the worst of circumstances. Mordecai would not bow to a bully, and Esther would not stand by and let that bully hurt the people she loved. They both enlisted the help of others and were willing to be enlisted to help others! Mordecai asked Esther for help, and she, in turn, asked he, all the Jews in the city of Susa, and her handmaidens to fast before she enlisted the king's help. All of their fasting and prayers were working. God was orchestrating circumstances while Esther carefully planned and boldly confronted her bully.

If you are being bullied, badgered, ridiculed, or threatened, tell someone, actually lots of people. Make sure that some of those you tell have the authority and power to help you: principals, teachers, parents, counselors, pastors, priests, employers, supervisors, human resources departments, police officers, and/or friends. Ask the Lord who to enlist and how to proceed from there. Remember, he is opening doors, but you have to go through them. You will feel alone, but as you ask for help, you will find what Esther discovered, God was there all the time.

Have you told the people closest to you that you are being bullied? Circle one below:

Yes   No

If your answer were no, why haven't you told them? List your reasons here:

If the answer were yes, list the names (or your relationship to each person) of those whom you have asked for help. Examples could be mom, dad, wife, husband, friend, sister, brother, cousin, uncle, aunt, friend, and so forth.

Have you told someone who has the power or authority to do something about the bullying?

Yes   No

If so, list their names or relationship to you. Examples would be parent, employer, supervisor, union representative, human resources representative, teacher, counselor, principal, police officer, district attorney, and so forth.

If you have not told someone about the bullying, what are the reasons for your hesitation to share that information?

Bullying may take a while to stop (the reason for the title of this book, *Forty Minutes or Forty Days*). Knowing that, are you willing to be patient, like Esther, and not give up, but look for the perfect opportunity to enlist the help you need?

How do you like the clever way that Esther trapped and exposed Haman?

What do you admire about Esther's guardian, Mordecai, and the way he quietly stood up to his bully Haman by not bowing to him?

Was Esther wise, or did she take too big a risk to enlist the king's help and support?

What would have been the outcome if Esther had passively stood by and let the bully Haman carry out his horrible plan?

What do you like best about the story of Esther?

How does Esther's story of faith, patience, cunning, and speaking up to enlist help give you hope or ideas for stopping your bullies?

MY PLAN OF ACTION

CHAPTER 12

Evaluate Your Life Goals and Live Them

God Gave This Life to You;
Don't Give It Away to Anyone
Don't Keep Looking Over Your Shoulder;
Your Future Is in Front of You

Let your eyes look straight ahead, fix your gaze directly before you. Make level paths for your feet and take only the ways that are firm.
—Proverbs 4:25–26

> Kindness is a language, which, the deaf can hear,
> and the blind can see.
>
> —Mark Twain

The quote by Mark Twain was posted on one of Tim Tebow's past websites on July 13, 2015. I included it here because it describes the former football player's philosophy on and off the field. Tim is a winner of two NCAA national football championships and first-ever sophomore Heisman Trophy winner of the James E. Sullivan Award as the nation's most outstanding amateur athlete in any sport. He was also the number-one draft pick in 2010. But by far, Tim Tebow's greatest accomplishment has been the way he inspires others.

Between games, Tim was known to visit terminally ill kids in the hospital, spend time with their families, and then invite them all on the sidelines of his upcoming games. Tim had a vision beyond football. That vision came to life in 2010 when he formed the Tim Tebow Foundation, which he says exists to bring faith, hope, and love to those needing a brighter day.

Tim's foundation builds Timmie's Playrooms in children's hospitals, provides life-giving surgeries for children in the Philippines, and offers grants for families choosing to adopt international children with special needs. Tim's career is still in sports, and he has since been involved in baseball and is a college football analyst on SEC. Tim's book, *Through My Eyes,* was named the number-one sports book of 2011 and the best-selling religious book of 2011.[1]

So why is Tim, a successful man, in a book about bullying? Like you, he experienced being bullied. Attention by the media shifted from his football career and touchdowns each game to what Tim did in the end zone after each touchdown. As Tim ran into the end zone with the football and the crowd jumped to their feet cheering, Tim stopped, knelt, and bowed his head to thank

God in a simple prayer. That one humble gesture set him apart. The bullies singled him out and attacked.

Why would the media, other sports figures, and fans repeatedly criticize and find fault with one quiet moment glorifying God? The fact is that some people were jealous of his talent and success, offended by his faith, or just irritated because they did not like it. These may be the same reasons you are being bullied today.

Take courage and inspiration from a guy who has taken repeated hits from the media just for thanking God in public. His video, found on his website and YouTube, has a very clear message. Here is some of what can be found on that clip. These may be his words to you:

> It is not going to be easy. There are going to be a lot of people telling you, you can't, that you shouldn't that you won't, that you couldn't. But you can because we serve a big God and your goal should be as big as the God you serve. You don't know when you are in your fourth quarter. You don't know how much time you have left. Are you ready? Are you willing to finish strong?[2]

You are never too old to set another goal or dream a new dream.
C. S. Lewis

Tim Tebow is a good example in this chapter of someone who went for his dreams and thanked his Lord along the way. He also made many children's dreams happen, as mentioned here and seen on his website. But he had to keep his mind and body trained on a personal vision for his life. He turned a deaf ear to his bullies, never being sidetracked or discouraged by them. Tim's newest book released is entitled *Shaken: Discovering Your True Identity in the Midst of Life's Storms.*

What are you discovering about your identity and your own

dreams? Where are your goals? How will you accomplish them? Your plans may be as short term as this week or as long term as a year or twenty years from now. Throughout this book, you have thoughtfully read, written, and answered important questions so you are equipped to break loose from bullies! Part of this Break Free Method is being able to take back your life from those who disrupt it!

When I ask clients to write down their dreams or goals, many have told me that they don't have any. This is usually the case for those who have been ridiculed, passed over, criticized, or physically abused, often enough to lose hope or try to function without it. A goal is simply a dream with a plan. If you can direct your attention on what fulfills you, no matter how small or great the goal, your self-worth rises, and you become occupied with what is important to you!

So in case you are at a loss to find your dream, which may become your goal, I have made a list below. Notice some are as small as hobbies or as grand as major achievements. Remember, also occasionally a hobby later becomes a major achievement! These are just some examples to help you get started writing in your plan of action. Use any of these, or make your own list. However, try to not limit or edit yourself.

You don't have to be the best at something to enjoy it! I know musicians who stopped playing instruments they loved because someone they knew happened to play better than they themselves did. There are and will be great football players. Tim Tebow was just one of them. Somewhere, there will always be someone better. If he had worried about that, he could never have played the game he loved so well!

Circle the dreams or goals you have considered, already done, or would like to accomplish now or sometime in your life:

- Inventing
- Designing

- Learning how to ride a horse
- Learning how to ride a skateboard, skis, or surfboard
- Learning a different language
- Building a rocket, boat, airplane, or something else
- Becoming a scientist
- Playing an instrument
- Singing in a choir or band or having a solo singing career
- Landscaping, gardening, or farming
- Taking painting classes or becoming an artist
- Becoming an amateur or professional photographer
- Being part of a team or becoming a professional athlete
- Competing in an athletic event
- Becoming a runner, wrestler, tennis player, swimmer, and so on
- Learning how to ride a bike or becoming a cyclist
- Making a goal in soccer
- Becoming an architect, engineer, or builder
- Becoming an author or journalist
- Writing poetry
- Becoming a Bible teacher, pastor, nun, or priest
- Traveling to one new place this year
- Traveling around the world someday
- Joining the Peace Corps
- Becoming a missionary
- Helping the poor or disadvantaged
- Joining the Boy Scouts, Girl Scouts, or the armed forces
- Becoming a baker or learning how to bake
- Becoming a chef
- Bodybuilding
- Going to college or graduate school
- Becoming a teacher
- Learning to sew
- Learning how to build or fix things that break
- Becoming a carpenter

- Learning how to dance or becoming a dancer
- Getting physically fit or becoming a personal trainer
- Learning how to hit a baseball or make a basket with a basketball
- Learning how to get organized
- Learning how to weld or becoming a welder
- Learning how to make stained glass
- Becoming a doctor, nurse, or dentist or having a career in the medical field
- Discovering something
- Investigating something
- Collecting something
- Breaking a world record
- Becoming a layer, judge, politician, or president of the United States
- Learning how to program computers
- Training to be an Olympic athlete
- Learning how to act in a play or movie
- Writing a play or skit
- Entering a contest
- Winning the Nobel Prize
- Winning the Pulitzer Prize
- Winning an award for something you would love to do or love doing now

One example of someone who has been able to rise above and beyond his bullies and live his dreams, helping thousands understand the value of being kind, is Nick Vujicic. He travels around the country, giving talks to churches, organizations, and schools. The kids especially respond to him as he stands on a table before them, walking back and forth as he talks. He stands balanced with only two protruding toes attached to one side of his torso to stabilize him. He has no arms or legs.

Nick has a warm, funny, charismatic personality. He is a

handsome guy with a winning way about him that draws people. He is also straightforward, challenging his audiences to be kind and stop bullying. His book, *Life without Limits*, tells how, as a boy, he tried to avoid being hurt by other kids at school. "On my good days I won them over with my wit, my willingness to poke fun at myself, and by throwing my body around the playground. On my worst days I hid behind the shrubbery or in empty classrooms to avoid being hurt or mocked."[3]

Nick explains to students in his presentations how he tried to commit suicide because of all the mean things kids said and did to him when he was a boy. He tells the student body, "You look at me, and think, 'Wow, those guys must to be heartless to bully someone with no limbs.' But why would you bully or tease anyone. We all have something wrong with us." Nick's video *Life without Limits* and his presentations on bullies can be seen on YouTube.

Nick's advice to kids in the assemblies, as he pats his Bible with his toe, is to be compassionate with one another and not tease anyone for any reason. His comfort to victims of bullies is at the heart of what he calls, "the three truths I needed to come to in my life: truth of my value, truth of my purpose, and truth of my destiny." These can be your truths today.

Nick, as you can guess, is a compelling, motivational speaker and author. He encourages people to care but also to discover their potential, not their limitations. (Search YouTube for "Nick Vujicic surfing.") His ability to bring out the empathy and best in people is his gift. He tells students he is in the Guinness World Book of Records for the number of hugs he has given in one year. He hugs people by leaning into them and letting them wrap their arms around him. Creating kindness is a strong antidote to the world of bullying.

This last chapter in part I was written to pull away your concentration from your bullies and put it back on your chosen destination. A shift in your thinking could help heal your mind, heart, and spirit from the awful effects of being bullied. There are, of course, painful, emotional scars and memories, but they don't need to stay open as fresh wounds. Taking back your life and future is like good medicine and a gradual healing salve on those hurts.

As you turn your eyes on God and what you are going to do, there is no place for bullies in that picture. You can do everything you have read and written in this book by staying focused on God's truth for you rather than the bullies' lies about you. This is your turn to begin writing the next chapter in your life. Do you remember *The Secret* in the preface of this book? The secret is that *your story is not over.*

You will now be writing for the last time, taking your own personal inventory and making your plan of action. You have the chance to evaluate what you want and how you want it. Whether breaking free from bullies took you forty minutes or you are finishing your forty days, this is your own program. Use it, look back at it, and keep moving forward with it.

Bullies will always be around, but you know how to handle them and break free from their control over you, now. Finish your Break Free in Forty with your Forty Devotionals to Fortify Your Soul! But before you do, here is my gift to you, a poem to stand at the door of your thoughts when old fears and bad memories try to trespass. God bless you, my friend.

Out of My Way

I still hurt from the mean words,
Wondering why they were said,
And horrifying pictures
Still running through my head.

You stole my happy moments
Every single day.
I lost my hope and future,
For you stood in the way.

Then I saw Jesus's bullies,
Laughing at him by the cross,
So sure they controlled his destiny.
Had they won? Had he lost?

A risen Savior, an empty tomb,
Too much to do to stay!
He lives, and so do I,
No bullies in our way.

This is your opportunity to write down your thoughts, hopes, and dreams. You can now begin focusing on what you want rather than what bullies allow you. When that happens, a whole new life emerges. Remember, God has gifted you, loved you, and called you. Look to the one that made you and equips you.

Note: Your goals may change as you grow and change through the years, but that does not mean you can't have hopes and dreams at every stage of your life! Start getting your life back on track as you put your thoughts down on paper today!

If you could do anything, what would it be? (You may want to write down the ideas you circled from the list of goals in this chapter or start a new list here!)

What are some of the talents or gifts God has given you?

Who are some of your heroes from the Bible and why?

Who are your heroes in literature or film (movies, TV, and so forth) and why?

Who are some of your heroes in real life and why?

If you had no bullies, what would you like to do this week that you cannot do when they are around you?

What are your favorite things to do whenever you have time to do them?

What is the most exciting or interesting activity you look forward to?

What have you learned about yourself and how to break free from bullies while reading this book?

MY PLAN OF ACTION

PART II
Daily Devotionals

Forty Devotionals to Fortify Your Soul

Scripture has the power to penetrate the soul; it refreshes the spirit, changes the mind, and strengthens the heart.

To the Jews who had believed him, Jesus said, "If you hold to my teaching, you are really my disciples. *Then you will know the truth,* **and the truth will set you free**.
John 8: 31

DAY 1

My flesh and my heart may fail but God is the strength of my heart and my portion forever.

—Psalm 73:26

Seabiscuit was a famous little racehorse who made a name for himself during the Great Depression of the 1930s. Seabiscuit outran thoroughbreds that stood taller and moved more gracefully than he. When he ran, his legs flailed out to the side, looking comical. Laura Hillenbrand, the author of *Seabiscuit: An American Legend*, said that horsemen called his type of running an egg-beater gait, a flailing motion with his left foreleg, as he swung it forward, as if swatting flies.[1] Short and stout, Seabiscuit didn't look like he belonged on a racetrack. But he ran with such power and determination that he became the champion and won the love and admiration of a whole country. Later when he died, they did an autopsy and discovered an enormous heart in that little horse.

Do you ever think you are different than others as if you don't quite fit in with everyone else? Maybe you are tired of trying. Good! Stop trying and start running your own race! Do what Seabiscuit did. Use your God-given gifts, and do what you do best. Apparently that little horse never compared himself to the larger, stronger competitors. He just pulled away from the pack and won his own race! Maybe you are facing opposition and obstacles, like bullies. They point out your shortcomings. When that happens, remember you have an inner quality that gives you power. Seabiscuit surprised everyone, and so will you! He stayed in his own lane and did what he did best - win!

When you lose faith, recite the verse above, "God is the strength of my heart." You might not feel like you can put one foot in front of the other, yet he pulls you up and gives you heart. It is as if your God is cheering you at the finish line, calling, "Just look at me. Don't look to the left or to the right. You can do this. I know it, because I know you better than you know yourself. You see, I am your creator."

The Race

Lord, Jesus, you are the strength of my heart.
I want to leave doubt behind
And run my very own race today
With only you in mind!

DAY 2

Get rid of all bitterness, rage and anger, brawling and slander, along with every form of malice. Be kind and compassionate to one another, forgiving each other, just as in Christ God forgave you.

—Ephesians 4:31-32

I remember cleaning out a garage one afternoon. By the time I was done, I had dust and grime in my hair, clothes, and shoes and covering my face and arms. I was sweaty, and my clothes stuck to my skin.

I threw my clothes in the hamper and jumped in the shower. The warm, clean water, shampoo, and soap never felt so good. What I didn't even think of doing was reaching back into that hamper and putting back on dirty socks and buttoning up grungy, sticky, smelly garments I had just peeled off. Instead I got dressed in crisp, clean clothes! Then I was ready to relax!

Rehearsing every injustice and becoming enraged over what someone has said or done is like rummaging through the dirty clothes hamper, dragging unwanted, greasy rags and putting them back on yourself. Why would you want to do that? Long after bullies have left the scene in your life, their words and abuse play back in your head. You cannot help that or stop that. But seething anger and rage can easily turn to bitterness. Then the intrusive thoughts hold you hostage. Ask God to help you forgive, and let go of the past and fill your mind with his goodness.

If you can keep the picture that the apostle Paul describes in the above verse, you can leave the unwanted filth and reach for the fresh, new life that Christ offers. You will feel so much more refreshed when you dress out your life so you become renewed in him.

Bitterness
A grudge is like a pain
That will not go away,
An unforgiving heart's resolve,
That anger is here to stay.

DAY 3

A troublemaker and a villain, who goes about with a corrupt mouth, who winks maliciously with his eye, signals with his feet and motions with his fingers, who plots evil with deceit in his heart-he always stirs up conflict. Therefore disaster will overtake him in an instant; he will suddenly be destroyed-without remedy.

—Proverbs 6:12–15

Some people are known as troublemakers. These bullies hang together and gang up on others. This verse is very descriptive about their tactics. They signal each other with a wink of an eye or a gesture. They have corrupt mouths, plot evil in their hearts, and stir up conflict. They think they are clever just because they are sneaky. And they assume they have the power because they work together and outnumber their victims. What bullies don't think about is how quickly disaster can overtake them. And it can come unexpectedly.

Have you ever been to the desert? It is usually a desolate place where cactus can grow in abundance and snakes and other reptiles move across the hot sand, unseen. Most of the time nothing interrupts this silent world. But occasionally, after a downpour of rain, a flash flood comes rolling through the whole area with the power of a freight train. Nothing can stop it. Weather and news alerts warn people to be aware. The danger is imminent.

God is warning bullies in this verse that disaster will suddenly overtake them with destruction that has no remedy. This desolate place where you find yourself, when faced with bullies, seems like miles of desert with no help in sight. But remember, bullies have their day but will not always have their way. God gives this warning so bullies have time to change. And he is encouraging you, no matter what change is coming!

DAY 4

Being strengthened with all power according to his glorious might so that you may have great endurance and patience….

—Colossians 1:11

One of the best movies dealing with teenage bullies is an old one, *The Karate Kid*. It came to the theatres back in 1984. It has since become a classic often seen on TV. Daniel, the main character, was a teenager who moved to a new city with his mother and found himself the target of bullies, members of a karate dojo whose teacher was also a bully. A patient and proficient karate expert, a Japanese American handyman at his apartment building, rescued and coached Daniel.

Nothing was quite as it seemed in the movie. The short, seemingly ordinary handyman was really a karate expert. The chores he gave Daniel to do around his home, for example, painting the fence or waxing the car, unknown to Daniel, were really exercises in training for karate. Daniel learned there was power in self-control and inner strength that would lead him to victory over those he once feared.

God knows who your bullies are and the strange new place in which you find yourself, today. Endurance and patience are not the same as simply tolerating abuse. Endurance is character that has steeled itself against being worn down. And patience is the ability to hold steady without reacting. God knows the victory he has planned for you and things are not always as they seem. You are in his training arena so look for the ways you are "being strengthened with all power according to his glorious might."

DAY 5

I will be glad and rejoice in your love, for you saw
my affliction; you knew the anguish of my soul.
And have not handed me over into the hand of
my enemy; you have set my feet in a spacious place.
—Psalm 31:7–8 (NKJV)

Have you ever been to a national park like Yellowstone, Sequoia, or Yosemite? The forests spread out in every direction for miles. They are thick, and branches occasionally block sunlight where trees grow side by side. If you are a backpacker, you can easily get turned around and feel closed in on every side, unsure which way is out. After hiking through miles of forests, suddenly you might step out into a lush, green meadow. It can feel so spacious and inviting. You just want to break loose and run through the grass! You can look up at the sky with white, billowy clouds rolling overhead and feel sunshine on your face. You are able to see all around without obstacles and have plenty of elbow room.

This is how the psalmist felt after being so closed in and trapped by bullies. He says, "(God) You have not shut me up in the hand of my enemy; you have set my feet in a wide place."

What is the spacious, wide place of safety God is opening up to you right now so you are able to escape the lost or trapped feeling of being bullied? Is it a change in schools, different job, new friends, relationship, or even a new town? Keep your eyes open, and search for a safe place where you are able to move freely. God has set your feet in a wide place.

A Wide Place
Lord,
I am never so lost that you can't find me,
Not so trapped that I can't get away.
You clear the way ahead and behind me.
You give me room to maneuver today!

DAY 6

In the morning, Lord, you hear my voice; in the morning I lay my requests before you and wait expectantly.

—Psalm 5:3

The psalmist tells you something about training yourself in the secret art of faith and patience. Faith is the belief in what you can't see, and patience is the ability to wait for it. But look closely at how the person praying to God waits. He rises early in the morning, looking for God. (The verse repeats this.) Then he declares that God "hears my voice," which means he trusts his creator to listen and he is willing to talk to his God out loud. The man then details his requests to God as he prays, "I lay my requests before you."

Finally the most important part of the training is when the person praying learns to wait with patient anticipation. The psalmist's eyes are not on the bullies' activities, but on his king. He will wait for God to act or show him how to move, but he absolutely expects that to happen. He "waits expectantly." He is training himself every day so he is ready when God makes a move.

I live on a hill overlooking the ocean. One day I was looking out my window and saw a boat coming around Morro Rock toward the open sea. (Morro Rock is a 581 foot volcanic plug in the ocean that towers over the bay.) I noticed black, billowing smoke coming from the boat's stacks. Suddenly the vessel changed course and headed for the shore. The smoke got blacker, and I went to get my binoculars to see if the boat were in fact on fire. By the time I returned to the window with the binoculars, the boat had vanished.

I tried to convince myself that those on the boat were okay, but finally knowing I couldn't live with myself if people were drowning, I called the Coast Guard. To my surprise, a member of the Coast Guard arrived at my door with binoculars and a radio. He talked to a captain of one of their boats that sped along the coastline. The man in my living room directed the Coast Guard boat to the exact place where the phantom boat had disappeared. The official boat went to each of the few other fishing vessels in the area to question them. Unfortunately I was the only one who saw the boat in distress.

I was feeling embarrassed and foolish until the officer beside me received a call that, in fact, a boat was having problems and had gone out to sea with the intention of testing the engines. When the vessel got in trouble (which was the black smoke I saw), it turned back around Morro Rock and returned to the bay. I apologized to the officer for bothering him.

He replied, "No, that was good. You have a vantage point here. You can see things we can't. We count on people to keep watch. Call us any time."

What if that struggling boat had capsized and I hadn't called for help because I doubted that the Coast Guard would come or I felt foolish for bothering them? God may be training you to trust him. If you are struggling and in trouble because of bullies, let God know your struggles. You are never bothering God by telling him your concerns or fears. Lay all your requests out before God early in the morning, and wait and watch expectantly. You count on him to answer, and he counts on you to ask.

DAY 7

Everyone who is called by my name, whom I created for my glory whom I formed and made.

—Isaiah 43:7

"Created," "formed," and "called" are wonderful words. They are wonderful because they describe you! God claims you as his own when no one else will. He had a plan for you when no one else did.

Do you ever feel like you are invisible to other people? If you have been bullied, you may have felt forgotten and unimportant if bystanders pretended not to see what was happening. You may begin to question your own self-worth. You wonder whether anyone really cares or knows you.

God, however, has a perfect view of you. He knows how you feel and what you have gone through. He knows why he made you in his own image. Your creator smiles with full confidence in your ability to glorify him. If Almighty God created you to radiate his character, he must have designed a unique future for you, where you can best display his love.

Insert your name in place of the word "everyone" in the above verse. Then recite that verse aloud several times in a twenty-four-hour period. See if it changes how tall you stand or influences how boldly you walk your path today.

Called and Created
Lord, you called us by name.
We were created each by you.
Not one of us is the same.
You predicted. You knew.

A living masterpiece by the artist,
We are each one of a kind,
The imagination of your heart,
We are your design.

DAY 8

Very early in the morning, while it was still dark, Jesus got up, left the house and went off to a solitary place, where he prayed.

—Mark 1:35

What do you think about doing on a cold winter morning when it is still dark out? Do you wish you could postpone the day ahead and just climb back under the warm covers and sleep? If you dread the day ahead because of bullies, then you may need to start early with the one who created the day, the Lord Jesus. When Jesus walked this earth, he arose while it was still dark and went out and found a quiet, solitary place where he could pray. He did this before the whole world woke up with its noise and demands.

The sweetest moments stolen away with Christ are not when you drag yourself out of bed to read your Bible and pray out of a sense of duty. They are the times you can't wait to run to him like a long-lost friend or loved one that will thrill you with every insight entrusted to you.

You know this devoted friend cares, listening intently with undivided interest as you pour out your thoughts. Those early hours in prayer will influence the entire day. Everyone you meet and everything you do will have a different meaning to you because you met with your beloved Savior first.

Now you will be prepared, strengthened, and certain you are not alone. What do you imagine the Lord might say to you tomorrow morning in the stillness as dawn breaks? Set your Bible, pad, and pen in your favorite place tonight. Then meet your friend Jesus tomorrow, writing down every word of hope from his heart to yours.

Early
A darkened morning has a quiet chill.
Leaves and grass are still wet with dew.
Sunrise unwraps the corners of the night,
As my day, Lord, begins with you!

I open the psalms, and there you are
With a promise I had not seen before.
I memorize the hope in each verse.
I am loved; I know it once more.

DAY 9

For you did not receive a spirit that makes you a
slave again to fear, but you received the Spirit of
sonship and by him we cry "Abba, Father." The
Spirit himself testifies with our spirit that we are
God's children.

— Romans 8:15–16

Abba is one of the easiest words for a Hebrew baby to say as he or she reaches arms up to a parent. The word "Abba" means daddy. Of course this is an irresistible sight for a loving father who then scoops his sweet child up into his arms. The child locks little fingers around Daddy's neck and rests safely in his arms.

Don't you wish life was that simple? Though you can't feel your Heavenly Father's arms, he reminds you they are there. Bullies like to isolate their victims and make them believe that they are helpless and alone. Instilling fear in a person's heart is their way of maintaining control.

Fear says, "Pay attention to me. Let me take hold of you." Your tender and faithful Heavenly Father says (Rom. 8:15–16 in today's language), "Climb up into my arms and let me hold you. You can call me Daddy because you are without question my child. You don't have to go back to being habitually afraid anymore. Pay attention to me until my Spirit comforts your spirit deep inside your heart with the reassurance that you are indeed mine."

Abba
Lord, I am frightened of what I do not know.
The danger looms large up ahead.
Let me climb up in your strong arms
And look to you instead.

DAY 10

In the shelter of your presence you hide them,
from the intrigues of men; in your dwelling you
keep them safe from accusing tongues.

—Psalm 31:20

When a storm suddenly breaks out, everyone runs for shelter. What a contrast between standing out in the wind, exposed to lightning and pouring rain, or finding a safe, warm protected place to rest. As noted in previous chapters, bullies may plot, but God is the one with the plan. The mean people make lots of noise accusing and slandering. But in the presence of God, there is peacefulness, a protection for the mind and soul.

Spend time with God today and read Psalm 31. Like many of the psalms, this one is all about bullies and all about God. The contrast is striking. Hide your heart in the shelter of his presence, and you will stop listening to the noise of the storm and the accusing bullies.

The Sheltering Presence
He is a mountain the enemy cannot scale,
A waterfall too powerful to hold back,
The great Rock in whose shadow I rest.
He hides me and leaves not a track.

DAY 11

But the wisdom that comes from heaven is first of all pure; then peace-loving, considerate, submissive, full of mercy and good fruit, impartial and sincere. Peacemakers who sow in peace raise a harvest of righteousness.

— James 3:17–18

What is the opposite of bullies? It is not victims. The opposite of bullies are individuals who resemble Jesus. Look at the list above: pure, peace-loving, considerate, submissive, full of mercy and good fruit, impartial, and sincere. This is wisdom straight from God.

Those passages are not telling you to be passive nor to submit to people who terrorize. Instead it is all about staying connected to Christ and watching the cause and result. When you submit to only the desires of God, you respond to others differently. You become the peacemaker planting seeds that become a harvest of righteousness.

Sow Peace; Raise Righteousness
Mercy and peace grow
When we remove the bitter weed,
Open our hand with kindness,
And plant the seed.

DAY 12

...but they were scheming to harm me; so I sent
messengers to them with this reply: "I am carrying
on a great project and can not come down. Why
should the work stop while I leave it and go down
to you?"

— Nehemiah 6:2–4

Bullies love to sidetrack and intimidate you. Nehemiah understood this. But he wasn't going to let that happen. He waited and prayed to be able to rebuild the wall around his beloved city. He, his countrymen, and countrywomen had been in captivity for years. Once King Artaxerxes gave permission for Nehemiah to go home and rebuild the protective wall, nothing was going to stop him!

Bullies demand your full attention, and they want you to do only what they tell you to do. Nehemiah knew, if he came down off the wall and let the bullies hurt or distract him, he would never complete the project that was dearest to his heart. Don't waste time thinking about why bullies do what they do. Instead get busy doing the thing you love and God has put in front of you today.

Your Heavenly Father has a blueprint for your life, and some of that is what you are doing right now! Keep the bullies in your peripheral vision but not in your primary field of focus. Christ wants to take the lead and rivet your attention on something wonderful that can only be accomplished with your style and perseverance. The next time bullies demand you obey them, say to them or to yourself the words you heard from a very tenacious Nehemiah, "Why should the work stop while I come down to you?"

The Plan
Lord, when I am discouraged
And cannot understand,
Help me keep my eye upon
The ONE who has the plan.

DAY 13

But God chose the foolish things of the world to shame the wise; God chose the weak things of the world to shame the strong. He chose the lowly things of the world and the despised things-and the things that are not-to nullify the things that are, so that no one may boast before him.

—1 Corinthians 1:27–29

Years ago, I had the privilege of spending a full week being taught the book of John by the late, great Pastor Ray Stedman. I was with a group of Bible teachers, all preparing to go back in September and teach the gospel of John to our classes. We were from different cities and states. I will never forget a story he shared that is a perfect application for our Bible verse today!

This true story is about a great evangelist who shared the gospel across the United States in the 1800s. He was scheduled to speak to an Ivy League university. Some of the students were indignant that he would have the nerve to come and lecture them! So a group of young men stuffed some ripe tomatoes in bags, sat in the front row of the lecture hall together, and waited for the chance to humiliate him. I am sure, like all bullies, they were laughing, whispering to each other, and feeling justified that they were only going to give him what he deserved.

As the godly man made his way to the center of the stage, he was directly in front of the angry students. One by one, each man reached into his own bag, looking up into the face of his target. The evangelist suddenly looked down into their eyes. He pointed at them, stating, "Don't ever think that Jesus Christ don't love you because he do!"

The young men were baffled by the speaker's words and by the passion with which he delivered his speech. The tomatoes were never thrown. The proud bullies were humbled and listened awestruck to the entire message God sent the evangelist to give that afternoon. The good news needs to be shared with bullies, even if it is with broken English or poor grammar. God likes to surprise the world by using the most unassuming people for his purpose in his timing.

The guest speaker at that prestigious university preached in the slums and led a revival across Britain and the United States. We never will know the names of his bullies. However, we do know the name of his savior, Jesus.

Foolish Things?
Was it foolish for God to love us?
So much that he sent his Son?
Believing we would love him
And come?

John 3:16 says, "For God so loved the world that he sent his only, begotten, son, so that whosoever would believe in him would not perish but have eternal life."

DAY 14

Surely he will save you from the fowler's snare and from the deadly pestilence. He will cover you with his feathers, and under his wings you will find refuge; his faithfulness will be your shield and rampart. You will not fear the terror by night nor the arrow that flies by day.

— Psalm 91:3–5

Psalm 91 is a wonderful scripture to memorize from beginning to end. The vivid picture of a battle and God's protective presence in the middle of the chaos can be a comfort to anyone in trouble. Bullies put on a persona that can almost convince you they have the ability to be everywhere at once. You may become fearful that, wherever you go and whatever you do, you will be found out or seen by them and be put in danger. The fact is just the opposite.

Bullies fill the air with fear by bragging about all they will do. But they are limited to one place at one time. God, however, surrounds you, goes before you, and is behind you. He "has your back," so to speak.

Memorize the above psalm and say it aloud every day this week, even if you have doubts it is true. It will counter all the loud lies that bullies throw like arrows. You will find that bullies are limited in time and space. Your God, however, is not!

My God is my General and my King.
He leads and surrounds me with care.
When war breaks out around me,
He is there.

DAY 15

When the Gentiles heard this, they were glad and glorified the word of the Lord. And as many as had been appointed to eternal life believed. And the word of the Lord was being spread throughout the region. But the Jews stirred up the devout and prominent women and the chief men of the city, raised up persecution, against Paul and Barnabas, and expelled them from their region. And they shook off the dust of their feet against them and came to Iconium. And the disciples were filled with joy and with the Holy Spirit (NKJV).

—Acts 13:48–52

Have you, like Paul and Barnabas, ever been expelled from something or somewhere? Maybe it was from a class, club, job, or a sport? Maybe you were not expelled, but you were excluded from a group? How did Paul and Barnabas keep from being discouraged and emotionally damaged? Verse 48 gives us the answer.

God had very recently helped the two men share Christ with Gentiles who were excited about the Word of God! The apostles shared their gospel. The Gentiles shared their joy!

When bullies try to exclude or push you out, keep focused on what and who is important. If you want so badly to be with the popular or successful people, you ignore those God has put into your life needing and wanting your attention. That is where you will thrive and have a sense of purpose and joy. Other people's excitement can be intoxicating.

The Gentiles were so happy to hear they were included in God's kingdom that the apostles didn't care if they themselves were excluded from the social network of their day. Paul and Barnabas shook the dust off their sandals toward the bullies. The two men turned their attention to the people, whose joy in Christ carried them to the next adventure in their lives.

Exclusion
Lord, many turn their backs,
Ignore you, or walk away.
Others value your company
And ask you to stay.

DAY 16

The Lord said, "Go out and stand on the mountain, in the presence of the Lord, for the Lord is about to pass by." Then a great and powerful wind tore the mountains apart and shattered the rocks before the Lord, but the Lord was not in the wind. After the wind there was an earthquake, but the Lord was not in the earthquake. After the earthquake came a fire but the Lord was not in the fire. And after the fire came a gentle whisper.

—1 Kings 19:11–12

The prophet Elijah had just come from an exciting event where he challenged the priests of Baal to call on their god to consume a sacrifice, and he would call on his God to do the same. Then he told all the people to decide once and for all which god they worship. (His nation had become a country of idol worshippers.) The Baal priests called on their god. They cried to Baal (said to be the god of fire) and even cut themselves in an attempt to get their god's attention. But nothing happened.

Then Elijah prayed to the Almighty God. Flames came down from heaven, not only burning up the sacrifice but also licking up the water around it. What a sight!

Sometimes after the most amazing victories in the Lord, the enemy attacks the hardest. That is what happened to Elijah. Jezebel, the king's wife, a narcissistic bully who was also a Baal priestess, led her henchmen on a nationwide hunt for the prophet. So Elijah ran for his life. He was alone, discouraged, and tired.

Suffering from a deep depression, Elijah asked God to take his life. He was done! The man of faith was full of doubt. He may have wondered if God were in charge why bullies continued to pursue him. So exhausted and afraid, Elijah ran into the wilderness until he couldn't go any farther. There he stopped to rest and fell asleep. An angel woke him and gave him something to eat.

Elijah traveled to the Mount Horeb. God sought him out. "What are you doing here?" When God asks you questions like that, it is not because he doesn't know. It's because he wants you to examine your motives and actions. These may be thoughts or impressions he gives you, just as striking as the audible words Elijah heard from God's mouth.

God may be putting this question to you today, "What are you doing here." He knows you are worn out. Bullies may have chased and intimidated you to the point that you are ready to give up. But don't! God wants you rested, nourished, and encouraged. You need a quiet place with a quiet peace of mind. Then listen as he whispers in your heart his most loving words to you. He will tell you truth and what you long most to hear. Like Elijah, you might need to know that you are not as alone as you think.

Elijah complained to God, "I am the only one left, and now they are trying to kill me too." Then Elijah was told, "Go out and stand on the mountain in the presence of the Lord, for the Lord is about to pass by."

A powerful wind, earthquake, and fire shattered the rocks and shook the mountain all around and under him. But God was not in any of those frightening and cataclysmic events. God came in the still, small voice that followed.

And once again, God questioned him, "What are you doing here?"

Elijah poured out his trouble to God again! This time God gave him instructions and the encouragement he needed most. God announced he was preparing to send Elisha to help Elijah in his work. He would be a prophet and a good friend. Then Elijah's Lord shared the surprising news, "I have seven thousand people that have still not bowed their knee to Baal."

When you are sure you are alone, God points out you are not. When you are ready to give up, he gives you rest and hope. When you are battling bullies, God gets you away with him to remind you who has the power. Significant moments are not in the wind, earthquakes, fire, or any terrifying events you experience today, but in the whispers of God.

The Wind, The Earthquake, The Fire, and The Whispers of God

I wanted to run away from life.
I felt so all alone,
I was tired of trying; I gave up the fight.
God can't use me. I'll just go home!
Then God asked me, "What are you doing here?"
And he let his holy wind
Move around me and remind me
The greatest power still comes from him.
Did he know my world was shaken?
The ground had broken loose beneath my feet?
Did he guess that I was panicked?
That all my thoughts told me "retreat"?
Cleansing fire from heaven then burned away
All the lies bullies told in the past.
God surrounded me with an amazing peace
When the silence came at last …
He whispered, "Child, why are you here?"
He listened as no one would do!
"I'll bring you the friends; today's not the end.
And I'll never give up on you."

DAY 17

You, dear children, are from God and have overcome them, because the one who is in you is greater than the one who is in the world.

—1 John 4:4

One of the biggest mysteries in the Christian faith is how the Holy Spirit comes and lives inside the Christian. Jesus told the disciples before he was crucified that he was going back to his Father. He explained, if he didn't leave, the Holy Spirit couldn't come. Jesus breathed the Holy Spirit into their lives. The original meaning for Holy Spirit is "holy wind" or "breath." It also means "one who comes alongside."

Just as God breathed his own life-giving breath into the first human being in Genesis, so he breathes a holy, eternal breath into all who love his Son. The promised Spirit would comfort and teach the Christian all about Christ. The Holy Spirit reminds you of everything Jesus said (John 14.) Jesus told the disciples, because they could have his own Spirit, they would do even greater things than they had seen him do! (John 14:12).

This can give you hope that, if you are Christ's disciple, you have that Spirit and therefore that same power. Just as Satan never had power over Jesus when he walked on earth so Satan has no power over you. Remember, Jesus came intentionally to earth to go to the cross and die in your place for your sins. Until his Heavenly Father's appointed time to die and be raised, he walked this earth, handling bullies while helping people. He was not anyone's doormat, though he had his share of bullies. He was never a martyr. He was the Master.

When bullies push you around or threaten, it seems there is no escape. But if you love instead of hate, you have already overcome. Control is something you can either give to someone else or hand over to God. And as you look for God's opportunities, he will empower you to do great things with great faith because "Greater is he who is in you than the one who is in the world."

Greater

Lord,
Your power to overcome was greater
Than threats from bullies I knew.
I forgot to be afraid
When I drew my faith from you!

DAY 18

"You have heard that it was said to 'love your neighbor but hate your enemy.' But I tell you love your enemies and pray for those who persecute you."
—Matthew 5:43–44

This has to be one of the most difficult passages in scripture to do! Why would Christ ask you to do something so impossible and improbable? If bullies persecute you, why must you love and pray for them? Maybe because that is exactly what Jesus would do (as covered in our earlier chapters) and in fact did from the cross. "Father, forgive them for they know not what they do" (Luke 23:34).

"Forgiveness is a gift, but trust is earned" was at the heart of one of our chapters. But after all you have read in this book and written in your personal inventory and plan of action, you still may be understandably harboring hatred for those who hurt you.

Your mind's mantra may be protesting with "I can't!" as you even consider forgiving bullies. You rehearse the malicious words bullies said to you so you can remind yourself how bad the bullying really was or is and why you are justified in getting back at your tormentors. The protests in your head may go something like this, "I can't forgive. I can't forget. I can't let go. I can't stop thinking about it. I can't stand them. I can't ever be happy. I can't trust anyone ever again. I can't start over. I can't stop hating them. I can't do anything. I can't feel normal!"

The fact is that you may be absolutely right. Bullies have maligned or accosted you, which resulted in your feelings of helplessness. So how can you love or forgive those who have committed such heinous crimes against you? You can only do this when you love Christ more than you hate your enemies. Then you leave it in God's hands. If you receive the love God has for you, he will give you enough for others. You don't ever have to like bullies. You only have to love them!

The more you pray for enemies, the greater investment you have in their life change. Prayer for someone else nurtures kindness and releases you from a deep-seated loathing that would otherwise overwhelm you. You can't remove a bad memory, but you can let the one who made you make changes in the way you think about yourself and those who have hurt you.

Your "I can't" could very well turn and become "I can." "I can do everything through him who gives me strength" (Phil. 4:13).

I Can

I can learn because Christ is my teacher.
I can follow when he leads the way.
I can change for Christ made my features
And renews me each day.

I can forgive for I've started over
When there was no place to start
But to look in the depths of my Jesus,
To be freed by the love in his heart.

I can smile because he has blessed me.
I can hug others because I've been held
By a faithfulness that caressed me
And never failed.

All these things "I can"
Because he whispers in my ear
"I know, my child, that you cannot,
But I can, and I am here!"

DAY 19

A man of knowledge uses words with restraint and a man of understanding is even-tempered.

—Proverbs 17:27

A fool finds no pleasure in understanding but delights in airing his own opinions.

—Proverbs 18:2

Take a look at Proverbs 18:2. Have you ever been around people who brag loudly all the time and are inconsiderate of others? Crowd pleaser bullies are like that. Abusive people are unsure anyone will want to be around them without putting on a show for everyone. Frequently these bullies make fun of others as part of that show. People laugh and watch, but they hardly ever respect the abusers. Even if they act like they are friends with the bullies, there is little trust or loyalty.

Now read Proverbs 17:27, "By contrast this is a wise, careful and considerate person. He or she can be trusted." You aren't afraid this friend will fly into a rage or say something cruel on impulse. "A person of knowledge, restraint, understanding, and even-tempered." This is a friend that most people want in their lives. That is a safe person and someone who is usually admired. Be the Proverbs 17:27 individual, and when the bully is filling the air with toxic noise, remember that you are choosing your words and the time to use them.

Words
Wound or heal a heart
Cause thoughts to be anxious or calm
Only in my possession while I am silent
When I speak, they are gone.

DAY 20

The word of the Lord came to me, saying, "Before I formed you in the womb I knew you, before you were born I set you apart; I appointed you as a prophet to the nations." "Ah, Sovereign Lord," I said, "I do not know how to speak; I am only a child." But the Lord said to me, "Do not say, I am only a child. You must go to everyone I send you to and say whatever I command you. Do not be afraid of them, for I am with you and will rescue you," declares the Lord.

—Jeremiah 1:4–8

Amazing! How would you feel if God said that to you? What an assignment he was given! Picture this: a nation torn by civil war had stopped worshipping God and were making idols and worshipping them in his place. The citizens were bullying each other as well. Then a new power arose on the horizon, and the nation of Babylon marched across the pages of history. They were also idol worshippers, and they were going to invade Judah and take the people captive.

Jeremiah's job was simply to warn his people what was going to happen as a result of turning their back on God. He was about to tell a whole group of bullies that a bigger nation of bullies was about to invade their country. He wasn't going to be very popular after sharing that news! So God also told the prophet to encourage his rebellious people. God promised to bring them back home to be a nation again, after they had a huge time-out to think about their horrible behavior toward him and each other.

Jeremiah was most likely a teenager or in his early twenties. He probably felt like a little boy again! God knows before you know when fear is going to grip you. And he wants to help. So don't say, "I can't speak. I am only a child." God said this to Jeremiah and may be saying this to you. Because when bullies threaten, God sees a bigger and better picture of your life than anyone, including you, could ever guess. Memorize what God said in verse 8, "Don't be afraid of them for I am with you and I will rescue you, declares the Lord!" What God did for Jeremiah, he can do for you!

DAY 21

Blessed are the peacemakers for they shall be called children of God.

—Matthew 5:9

Do you know people who continually look for a fight? They pick at others and try to get an argument out of them. If you say something, they say just the opposite to make you look foolish. Their goal is to be "peace-breakers."

Being a peacemaker pleases God. He even calls you his own. You look and act like him when you are kind! You have probably heard relatives say, "You remind me of your dad when he was your age." Even if you are adopted, you may follow your mom's example and do things so similar that people would remark, "The way you do that is so much like your mom. I would guess you are her daughter!"

If you are considerate, even when bullies try to badger, other people notice the difference! And you are, in fact, being a peacemaker like Jesus was on earth. This proves to people you are like your Heavenly Father. Anyone can be cruel, especially if another is cruel to you first. But Jesus handled bullies without ever becoming one of them. He knows how to make you into a peacemaker, and your Heavenly Father points at you with pride and says, "That's my child!"

The world needs peacemakers
(Not the voice of an angry crowd)
Reasonable and compassionate,
Who will make God proud.

DAY 22

When a man's ways are pleasing to the Lord he makes even his enemies live at peace with him.

—Proverbs 16:7

Have you ever noticed that, the harder you try to please people who don't like you, the meaner they are to you? It is as if they know how much it means to you to be liked. That seems to give them power over you. This verse gives you an amazing secret combination to unlock the possibilities of getting an enemy to become a friend or at least live at peace with you.

The above verse talks about having a singular goal of pleasing God. Your Lord knows how to make your enemies live at peace with you. This is not a guarantee. It is, however, a possible outcome. The proverb in essence says, "God notices your intentions and your lifestyle and uses that to influence those who would otherwise hold you in contempt." God wants your attention, love, and respect. Don't waste your time trying to please enemies. Just focus on your creator. Then he can help you persevere so that bullies may be willing to stop fighting you.

Let me share an interesting picture to illustrate how enemies become friends. A barge floats in a bay where harbor seals and sea lions come to soak up the sun and rest. Most of the time, planks can't be seen for the mass of bodies. When a seal wants on the barge, he has to launch himself out of the water, up onto the little wooden island, and get past the bigger, dominant sea lions that fight them along the edge. The biggest, noisiest, and most aggressive males are those sentinels that guard the entrance to the family real estate.

The most humorous part of the barking, battle of the King of the Hill seal scenario, is when a sea lion sneaks up onto the barge and wiggles over the other seal bodies. Then the great guardians realize they have been beaten. The big boys accept the invaders as part of the gang and appear to become their friends. People are a little like these guys.

Bullies make a lot of noise, are territorial, and demand the attention and respect of the ones they see as outsiders. Sometimes when bullies realize they have nothing to fear and that those they are trying to intimidate will not back down, our verse comes to life, "The Lord makes even his enemies live at peace with him."

Lord, keep my focus on you,
Not on what others think of me,
'Til I persevere with kindness
And make a friend of an enemy.

DAY 23

He rescued me from my powerful enemy, from my foes who were too strong for me. They confronted me in my day of disaster, but the Lord was my support. He brought me into a spacious place; he rescued me because he delighted in me.

—Psalm 18:17–19

Someone is in big trouble. Notice all the problems: "my powerful enemy," "my foes who were too strong for me," and "they confront me in my day of disaster." The psalmist sounds very intimidated! Just when things look so bleak and overwhelming, the writer remembers what God has done in the past, "but the Lord was my support, he brought me into a spacious place and he rescued me."

Sometimes you may forget all that God has done for you in the past. Without that record in your mind, you will fear disasters today. Begin a journal this week, and record all the answered prayers you can recall and the actual date God helped you. Try to write in it anytime you notice he comes to your rescue, even when you forgot to pray about it. Record dates and events when God uses other people to help you. Jot down situations where the Lord removes obstacles, which is the same as saying, "He brought me into a spacious place."

Recording and remembering God's goodness to you keeps your mind strong and your heart full of faith. You might want to write on the first page of a journal or one of your plan of action pages the reason God has and will take care of you. Psalm 18:19 says, "He rescued me because 'He delighted in me.'"

DAY 24

Suddenly an angel of the Lord appeared and a light shone in the cell. He struck Peter on the side and woke him up. "Quick, get up!" he said, and the chains fell off Peter's wrists.

—Acts 12:7

One of the most exciting scenes in the New Testament is Peter's miraculous rescue by God when he was in prison in Acts 12. (Take a few minutes and read this action-packed chapter!) Peter was shackled to two guards, and while they slept, his chains fell off, and an angel led him to freedom.

Here is a little background on the situation. King Herod was one of the most infamous bullies in the New Testament. (He was both a narcissistic and a crowd pleaser bully type.) Herod wanted to be popular with the people (who most of the time hated and feared him) so he threw Peter in prison to please the crowds.

But scripture tells us the church "was earnestly praying to God for Peter." The angel appeared and told him to get up. He obeyed the angel. Jail doors opened by themselves, and guards slept. And it all seemed like a vision or dream to Peter. When he ran to the house of his friends, who he knew would be praying together that night, they could hardly believe their own eyes. God had released Peter from his bullies, his cell, and the ultimate bully, King Herod!

This event is something you could imagine seeing in a science fiction movie with all the special effects, except it really happened and not magically, but miraculously. God was working behind the scenes, answering prayers that rose up in the night from a band of believers. Prayer made all the difference. This is just as true for you today. You need to pray for those you hear are being bullied and ask for prayers for yourself if you are being terrorized or controlled by bullies. Others need to know when you are in trouble. That way you are really never alone.

Miracles are meant to increase faith. Peter might never have seen a miracle if his fear had overshadowed his faith. Imagine him telling the angel, "I don't know how you got in here, but I am going to stay. Things will just be worse for me if I leave. The bullies will really get mad and hurt me then." Bullies want you to feel trapped so they have access to you. But when you pray and have others praying for you, while you move away from the danger, God has a route and a plan of escape.

Go to Acts 12 and see how God dealt with Herod. Peter's only real danger was to believe in the bullies' power rather than the power of God. If you are being bullied, you need prayer and support of others. Then follow the angel's instructions to Peter, "Quick! Get up." And follow God to freedom.

DAY 25

Are not five sparrows sold for two pennies? Yet, not one of them will fall to the ground apart from the will of your Father. Indeed the very hairs of your head are all numbered. Don't be afraid; you are worth more than many sparrows.

—Matthew 10:29–31

Do you know how many sparrows fill the trees? Can you count the hairs on your head? Do you know how many hairs are on someone else's head? Do you even care? God does. He doesn't forget about the fallen sparrow. He has never forgotten about you! God pays attention to detail, and the details of your life get his attention.

Bullies want you to believe you are forgotten and abandoned by others. They want to have control and dominate. They hope you think no one watches what happens to you. But the opposite is true. God sees and cares about everything that touches your life.

I will never forget Wetheral Johnson, who founded the now worldwide organization, Bible Study Fellowship International, speak about her prison of war experiences. She was a missionary in China during World War II. A Japanese soldier put a bayonet to her throat. Her first thought was, "Nothing can touch me that does not touch my Lord Jesus first." Surviving in a Japanese concentration camp, she lived each day believing God was there too. She was "not forgotten by God." He was her life goal. She would still be a missionary, but it would be in a concentration camp.

Wetheral Johnson's life and ministry after the war touched and changed other people's lives around the world. She wrote Bible studies that still impact generations. Many cities around the world have at least one active Bible Study Fellowship International class. Her life counted, and so does yours.

The bullies do not imagine that God notices injustice. The Almighty overlooks nothing. The Lord sees and feels every abuse you experience. He also views a bigger picture of all you will do beyond today. Your life is worth so much more than bullies will let you see. Only God knows your importance, "Do not be afraid; you are worth more than many sparrows."

Whatever touches me touches Jesus.
Nothing happens that he fails to see.
My hurt or burden weighs heavy on him.
He was once broken for me.

DAY 26

I have seen a wicked and ruthless man flourishing
like a green tree in its native soil, but he soon
passed away and was no more; though I looked
for him, he could not be found. Consider the
blameless, observe the upright; there is a future
for the man of peace.

—Psalm 37:35–37

One of the most infuriating feelings comes when you have to watch mean people get what they want or do whatever they please seemingly without consequence. You wonder, "Where is the justice in that?" You might catch yourself even saying out loud, "That is not fair!" But this is not the end. God is writing the ending. That is his job and not yours. He has an interesting way of leveling the playing field over time, which may, or may not, be on this side of heaven. His timing is not always ours.

Research shows, as you saw in chapter 1, that many children who bully live a life of crime as adults. They end up in jail or prison. You see them now, but you probably won't see them later. You will go on to live the life you want, but they will probably be in and out of trouble, in one scrape or another most of their lives. The ones who do stay out of jail usually have few friends, as most people don't trust nor want to be around them.

The verse above compares the wicked to a flourishing tree in its native soil. In other words, the bullies look strongest when in their own environment (situations where they can bully), like huge trees that flourish with branches like arms spreading across the sky. They can easily dominate and overshadow you.

There was a huge pine tree that was dense and bushy, and it smelled fragrant. It looked strong and rugged and had withstood wind and rainstorms through the years. But a little insect, a beetle, began to eat away at it. The tree lost its needles and looked sparse, dry, and spindly. It was only a matter of time before it would be removed. The place the tree had been would be a patch of ground with no remnant of it left, only a memory. The writer of this psalm saw that happen to the man he described as ruthless. In fact, he looked and could not even find him.

God reveals what a true success story is in his economy. And he indicates what your examples are and why. "Consider the blameless, observe the upright; there is a future for the man (or

226

woman) of peace." Let the Lord handle your bullies so you don't become a bully (a bully-victim) by your own retribution.

While you move on with your life, bullies fade into memory (not from memory into memory) until one day you can say like the psalmist, "I looked for him, and he could not be found."

DAY 27

Humble yourselves, therefore, under God's mighty hand, that he may lift you up in due time. Cast all your anxiety on him because he cares for you.

—1 Peter 5:6–7

My private practice is on the Central Coast of California. Sometimes I take my therapy sessions outside of my office. My clients and I do what I call "beach therapy." Some people drive two and a half hours from San Joaquin Valley for a session or two, and the ocean is just what they need. We walk along the shore and talk. We listen to the waves crashing and whispering in the foam left behind. The wet sand gleams in front of us. The ocean breeze (or wind) is on our faces as the sun warms our backs. My favorite part of beach therapy is helping clients do exactly what Peter is trying to get us to do in the above passage, "cast all our anxiety on God."

I have clients pick up little rocks along the shore. We stop, and they repeat out loud their deepest concerns. They give each rock the name of their worry, sadness, or anger. Then one by one, the rocks are cast or skimmed across the water as far as they can throw. Their fear or their doubts drop into the sea, one by one. Does this solve their problems? No. But it gets the process going. Admitting there is a problem and being able to do something with it helps people get emotionally unstuck.

God loves your bullies, and God loves you. But you may doubt his love, if you are at the mercy of your assailants every day! Imagine for a minute you could pick up one rock on the shore for every day that you doubt your situation will ever change. I'll bet you would have a pocket full of rocks! Now picture that you hand them to your Heavenly Father, and he hands you a note in exchange. You unfold the paper, and it reads like a poem, "I will take these and give them to my Son, because he walked on earth and had his bullies too. He will know what to do with each of your doubts … he cares for you."

Doubts

Lord, I say, "Why me?"
Or I wonder, "What if?"
I ask, "Why now?"
Or "What could I have missed?"

Then you take my doubts
And pick out the ones
Needing critical attention.
Then you add up the sum.

And you hand them back
Wrapped in one promissory note,
For one love and one Savior,
One unfailing hope.

DAY 28

Jesus heard that they had thrown him out, and when he found him, he said, "Do you believe in the Son of Man?" "Who is he sir?" the man asked. "Tell me so I may believe in him." Jesus said, "You have seen him, in fact, he is the one speaking with you." Then the man said, "Lord, I believe." And he worshipped him.

—John 9:35–38

The above verse comes on the heels of an exciting event for a blind man receiving his sight by Jesus. However, the man never got the chance to look on Jesus's face right after being able to see. But what elation the man must have felt looking at the world for the first time! Sadly the very next episode involved interrogation, accusations, and rejection for him by religious rulers, the Pharisees. They refused to believe the man had been blind or that Jesus healed him. The Pharisees were prepared to dole out punishment to them both.

The day began when Jesus met the blind man and healed his eyes on the Sabbath. According to the laws of the Sabbath, work was to cease until the following day, or at least until sundown, when the Sabbath (Saturday) was formally considered complete. The religious rulers of Jesus's day had distorted God's law, which was intended to help people become rested and refreshed. However, the religious rulers turned the Sabbath into a catchall of regulations beyond what God had intended. Because of this, the Pharisees tried to accuse Jesus of working on the Sabbath, merely because he helped a blind man see.

The religious rulers harassed the man who had been healed and his parents. The bullies tried to get the man to turn on Jesus and deny he healed his sight. Pharisees bullied the entire family, making them afraid of being excommunicated, so to speak. When the Pharisees didn't get the answers they wanted and no charges could be leveled at Jesus, they threw the man with the new sight out of the temple. This had implications, such as separation for him from his whole religious community and losing the right to worship God in the temple or synagogue. That is when Jesus found him once again.

Bullies come in all sizes and stations in life. Some may be in organizations or institutions that hold positions of power over you. But this does not give them the right to overpower you! Any position of power should always carry with it a responsibility of fairness and justice. This was clearly not the case with most of the religious rulers of that day. The man with new vision spoke up to these bullies and never backed down.

Here are a few of the replies the newly sighted man made back to the Pharisees (his bullies) when they questioned him, "I told you already, and you do not want to listen. Do you want to hear it again? Do you want to become his disciples too? Now that is remarkable! You don't know where he comes from, yet he opened my eyes. We know God does not listen to sinners. He listens to the godly person who does his will. Nobody has ever heard of opening the eyes of a man born blind. If this man were not from God, he could do nothing." An attitude of gratitude certainly gave the man with new vision a lion's heart.

The interrogated man was thrown out of the temple for defending his right to tell the truth and for speaking up for Christ, even though he did not know all the facts of Jesus's identity! Jesus searched for, found the outcast, and identified himself so the man understood him to be the long-awaited Messiah. More than his sight, he was given a personal audience with the Son of God, also known with the designation, the Son of Man.

Jesus hears you when you stand up for him. He respects your right to stand up for yourself when you are wrongly accused. This remains true, even if your bullies are in a legitimate position of power.

The courageous part of this story is that the newly sighted man simply told the truth, challenged his bullies for being ignorant of the facts, and confidently began questioning them! (See John chapter 9 to read the whole amazing story in its entirety for more details!) The bold man with his new sight handled his bullies, and Jesus sought him out for a more personal relationship with himself. Stand up for Christ. He will do the same for you!

Lord, I will stand up for you,
Even when I can't see you here,
You did not hide from me. You died for me.
Even now you are near.

DAY 29

Those who live according to the sinful nature
have their minds set on what nature desires; but
those who live in accordance with the Spirit have
their minds set on what the Spirit desires.

—Romans 8:5

A young man was in the final minutes of a grueling wrestling match, and the score was tied. He was a senior in high school, wrestling in one of his last matches. His wrestling coach from his freshman year was sitting up in the stands. The young wrestler stood exhausted. He stopped wrestling, looking discouraged and perplexed, wondering what move he could make to score a takedown.

Suddenly a familiar voice shouted instruction from the top of the bleachers. Out of all the cheers and shouts, only that one voice seemed to get his attention. He instantly did exactly what the voice told him to do, and the boy's opponent was on his back with both shoulder blades on the mat. The young wrestler jumped to his feet, and the referee grabbed his arm and raised it above their heads. In a matter of seconds, the struggle turned to victory simply by obeying the voice of a trusted coach.

Your natural response to being bullied is fight-or-flight. When you can't do either, you are like the young wrestler who momentarily becomes paralyzed, not knowing what to try next. Reading God's Word daily is like having a coach in your mind and heart, instructing you with sound advice. (Try reading one psalm and one proverb every day.) The Holy Spirit reminds you of a verse you know, and you have hope and courage again. Almost instantaneously you know what God wants you to do, and you don't hesitate. That is how matches are won and victories are gained.

If you are unsure what your next move is, listen to your coach. He knows not only what will give you victory. He knows you. What is your coach telling you today?

DAY 30

At my first defense, no one came to my support, but everyone deserted me. May it not be held against them. But the Lord stood at my side and gave me strength, so that through me the message might be fully proclaimed and all the Gentiles might hear it. And I was delivered from the lion's mouth.

—2 Timothy 4:16–17

The apostle Paul wrote some of his letters to the churches he had founded while under house arrest in Rome. However this second letter written to Timothy was when he was imprisoned under Emperor Nero. The correspondence was probably penned from a dungeon. Paul spoke of being brought up on charges at a hearing, where all his friends seemed to have deserted him. Yet he used that horrible time in his life as a chance to share Jesus and to encourage other fellow believers who were being persecuted by Nero. How did he keep his focus on the content of what he wanted to say and off his bullies who tried him and his friends who left him?

"But the Lord stood at my side and gave me strength." When everyone else leaves, God doesn't. Sometimes he delivers you from harm, "from the lion's mouth," so to speak. And other times God simply stands at your side and gives you strength. Because you are never without him, you can afford to be bold. He has much to say through you. And he knows you have much to say for him.

How is God pulling you out of the mouth of a lion this week? How is he giving you strength when everyone else seems to be gone? When you feel like you have no one, the invisible one stays closest.

No One

Lord, I have no one
Who looks deep into my heart,
Who knows my fears and counts my tears,
Who understands and takes my part.
Lord, I have no one
Who will take me as I am
And let me share and show they care.
I need a smile, a hand.
Then I take your Bible,
And I read in every phrase
Your promises and miracles
Flowing from page to page.
At the cross, I see salvation
At the tomb, victory,
At the pool of Bethesda, a loving Lord,
Reaching out to me.
No one came to your birth but shepherds.
No one understood your Messiah claim.
Knowing the cost, you went to the cross,
Cried, "Forgive them"; Holding no one to blame,
I will not say, "I have no one."
When I cried, my Savior, you knew.
I put self-pity to rest; I have found the best.
Oh, I have someone. I have you.

DAY 31

He who digs a hole and scoops it out falls into the pit he has made. The trouble he causes recoils on himself; his violence comes down on his own head. I will give thanks to the Lord because of his righteousness and will sing praise to the name of the Lord Most High.

—Psalm 7:15–17

Trying to get even with someone or taking a little revenge is just like digging a pit and then falling into it. This verse gives the warning that trouble recoils on itself, like setting a trap to spring and accidentally stumbling into it. The teeth of the trap won't let go because it was intended for someone else! We may not recognize until it is too late that our hatred for others attacks our own mind and heart.

Gang violence is one of the best examples of the above verse. Paybacks never get caught up. When one group evens the score with another, it is never even. What began as loyalty and justice deteriorates quickly into losing one's own humanity for the reputation, "bully."

The psalmist seems to stand back and take stock of what is happening around him. He learns and decides to exchange his belief in his right to retaliate for a heart of thankfulness. He has a God who is the great leveler and Lord of all. Rather than shout and curse at his enemies, he chooses a heart that sings praises to his Lord God Most High.

Are you digging a hole or grave for someone? Are you planning trouble for the person or people you believe have caused you harm? Throw the shovel away, and turn around and go a different direction. Stop digging in the dirt! Choose instead to offer up a prayer of thanks to God for being the judge who will not overlook all that has happened to you. He weighs everything in the balance.

I want to climb out of this hole I am digging
And reach for the skies!
The air is fresher where dreams live
Than in the dark where hope dies.

DAY 32

But even if you should suffer for what is right, you
are blessed. Do not fear what they fear; do not be
frightened. But in your hearts set apart Christ as
Lord. Always be prepared to give an answer to
everyone who asks you to give the reason for the
hope that you have. But do this with gentleness
and respect, keeping a clear conscience, so that
those who speak maliciously against your good
behavior in Christ may be ashamed of their
slander.

—1 Peter 3:14–16

The apostle Peter knew all about fear. He wrote this letter to the church encouraging them not to be afraid. But Peter remembered a night when fear ruled his every thought. He was terrified of being arrested and possibly crucified, so he denied Jesus three times in a matter of minutes. Standing outside the trial of his beloved Jesus, Peter warmed his hands by a fire when a young woman recognized him as one of Jesus's followers. So did others. Fearing for his own life, Peter swore, "I tell you! I do not know the man!"

So how could Peter be so bold to tell new Christians not to be afraid of their bullies? The same night prior to his passionate denial, Peter fought courageously for Jesus in the garden. He cut off the ear of the servant of the high priest who came with soldiers to capture Jesus. But Peter's Lord took the sword out of his hand and eventually out of his heart.

If attacking an attacker is not how Jesus wants you to handle your bullies and being a silent believer incognito never works, then what are you to do? Peter said, "Be prepared to answer for the hope that you have." Peter was not spiritually, mentally, or emotionally ready for the unexpected the night of Jesus's arrest. That night was burned into his memory. He had lots of time since then to think about his past behaviors and an alternative plan of action. He was therefore well qualified to help others with their fear by the time he wrote this letter.

Peter knew how to equip the church and you to handle bullies. His method came straight from his living Savior. You are encouraged to answer bullies "with gentleness, respect, and a clear conscience." Peter knew Christ forgave him. But you and I will never know how haunted the disciple was by his own conscience. Peter experienced how powerful a force was fear. He didn't want you to make his mistakes. Be prepared. Have an answer for your hope "so that those who speak maliciously against your good behavior may be ashamed of their slander."

After being Christ's disciple, Peter spent most of his life sharing the gospel message. This, I imagine, included sharing the night of his greatest fears.

Peter struck out defending Jesus one minute and denied him the next. But God could still trust his disciple because he knew Peter loved him. Peter could help others who had the same struggles when faced with bullies. He had learned the importance of being ready, and encourages you with his advice for that moment when bullies try to attack you or the Lord you love. Be prepared. How are you preparing yourself to speak up to your bullies for the hope you have?

Forgiveness and Friendship
God,
Forgive my rage in the night,
Denials by a flickering flame.
Like Peter, you changed my heart
To speak up for you again!

DAY 33

Everyone should test their own actions. Then they can take pride in themselves without comparing themselves to someone else.

—Galatians 6:4

Sometimes you might be your own worst enemy! Think about it. When you pick on yourself, finding a flaw and exaggerating it, you become your own bully. This usually happens when you compare yourself with someone else. You start tearing yourself down because you think another person is smarter, more confident, more attractive, more talented, more successful, or more popular than you are.

God wants you to be inspired by other people, but not to be jealous of them. Inspiration compels you to work harder and be excited because of the possibilities. Jealousy eats at you. It corrupts, making you sick and discouraged. That unfortunately is the perfect recipe for the making of a bully.

How do you keep from bullying yourself or others? Reread your verse for the day. You are to test your own behavior and be proud of the gifts God has given you. You can use your talents to build others up and be a blessing. Comparisons are deadly. They make you dissatisfied or critical of someone else. You begin to feel sorry for yourself. Thankfulness and self-pity are mutually exclusive. You are not able to think both ways at the same time. Choose to be thankful and proud of your own abilities. Thankfulness creates peacefulness, fulfillment, and goodwill toward others.

Resist comparisons that result in character assassination. Then you will not be tempted to ridicule yourself or anyone else. Simply refuse today to become anyone's bully, including your own!

DAY 34

David said to Saul, "Let no one lose heart on account of this Philistine; your servant will go and fight him." Saul replied, "You are not able to go out and fight him; you are only a boy, and he has been a fighting man from his youth."

—1 Samuel 17:32–33

I looked out my window and saw two tiny birds dive-bombing a hawk that was at least four times their size. The majestic bird usually soars on the sea breeze above the hills and across the sky where I live. He is typically the unchallenged king of the sky and bird of prey. The hawk is the feathered predator other smaller creatures fear. He can be seen slowly circling high in the air, searching for rodents on the ground, swooping down, and then carrying them away in his clutches. But this afternoon, he would dive and dip, attempting to get away from the relentless attack of the little pests that would not let him rise above them.

The little birds forgot they were tiny. Maybe they were protecting their nests and babies, like the shepherd boy, David, who was defending his countrymen and his family in Israel against the Philistines. The biggest threat that intimidated Israel's entire army was Goliath.

The great Goliath, a giant of a man and a crowd pleaser bully, had terrified King Saul's army and Saul himself. Every day the mammoth man came out in front of the Philistine army and bragged he would fight any soldier Saul sent to him from the Israelite army. Day after day, the armies faced off, and everyone was petrified when they heard his threats and saw his humongous stature. But the boy David assured the king that God helped him fight lions and bears to rescue his lambs. The huge soldier Goliath was just another bear to David. What God had done for David in the past, God could do for David in the future.

Saul enlisted the help of a boy. And David enlisted the help of his God. The shepherd offered to fight the giant. And God fought for David. Your bullies may look and sound daunting, and you may feel small. But as David said, "Let no one lose heart." Read 1 Samuel 17 today for the exciting details of a giant bully and a young man with a few small stones and a great God!

Big Enough

Giants tower over you,
Making you feel small.
Underestimating your courage,
They take the biggest fall!

DAY 35

Yet Paul grew more and more powerful and baffled the Jews living in Damascus by proving that Jesus is the Christ. After many days had gone by, the Jews conspired to kill him, but Saul learned of their plan. Day and night they kept close watch on the city gates in order to kill him. But his followers took him by night and lowered him in a basket through an opening in the wall.

—Acts 9:22–25

What a humbling and terrifying experience for the apostle Paul that evening long ago. By day he was preaching the gospel and turning hearts to Christ. He had a loyal following of believers and his fame was growing. But by night, he was curled up in a ball with his head down while his friends lowered him in a basket. He was helpless and dependent on his buddies to not drop him. They smuggled him through a hole in the city wall and down the other side so he could escape his bullies.

Sometimes, actually most times, you need help when bullies plot against you. Others need to know and help if you are in danger. But you may think you can handle it or even deserve it. After all, before Paul met his Savior Jesus on the road to Damascus, wasn't he on a mission to jail every Jewish man or woman who professed Jesus as Messiah? I wonder if that went through his mind as he inched his way down the wall that night, "I bullied so many people because I thought they deserved it. Were they as scared as I am tonight? Did they hide in baskets? Do my bullies believe I deserve to be caught and punished too?"

The Lord Jesus changed Paul's heart, forgave him, and used him in a mighty way. Jesus may do that for your bullies or help you turn away from bullying. If you are being tormented or hunted by bullies, get support and let others help you as Paul's friends helped him.

DAY 36

In the shelter of your presence you hide them from
the intrigues of men; in your dwelling place you
keep them safe from accusing tongues.

—Psalm 31:20

An old saying went like this, "Sticks and stones may break my bones, but words can never hurt me!"

Unless you are able to ignore abusive words and never take them to heart, that statement is far from true! Words wound and linger in your thoughts until you feel undone, unless you shelter your mind in the presence of Almighty God! Memorize the above verse if you are the target of "accusing tongues." Say it aloud whenever you need it.

The verse in Psalms talks about "accusing tongues." Try not to be overly concerned people will believe gossip told about you by bullies. People may be fooled in the short term, but the way you treat others proves who you are. Here is a life truth: You cannot defend yourself against every lie, but you can live the truth. Wait and let your reputation and the way you live speak for you.

If someone asks you about a dark lie, shine a light using one phrase, "That is not true." Don't call the bullies "liars," or you may become the accuser. Instead stick with the facts. The fact is, "That is not true."

The biggest trap you can fall into is being afraid and convinced that others will doubt you and believe bullies. Keep your head high and take that fear to the Lord. Read through the psalms. Underline or jot down all the times the psalmist was maligned by his enemies. Then write what he believed God would do to right the wrong. He used pretty strong language and vivid imagery of what he hoped God would do to stop them.

You can be honest with God. But run to him, not to everyone you think has heard the gossip. God can right the wrong in his time. And you can live as if everyone knew the truth in the meantime.

Reputation
I will not run to defend my name.
I'll live my life as only I can.
Lord, you right the wrong. I will be strong.
You know who I am.

DAY 37

Hatred stirs up dissension, but love covers over all wrongs.

—Proverbs 10:12

Hatred reduces a person's worth. Love upholds the value of a person's worth. Hatred is loud and mean. Love is humble and kind. Hatred justifies the wrong that will be done. Love forgives the wrong that has already been done or will be done in the future. Hatred fills a person with rage. Love fills a person with joy. Hatred is a heavy burden that cannot be set down. Love lifts the burden off the bearer with strength enough to lift another person's burden as well.

When you have been bullied, it is normal and right to be angry. Scripture never says not to get angry (as we learned in our chapter "Forgive Bullies; Don't Trust Bullies"). Scripture only says Ephesians 4:26 (RSV), "Be angry but sin not." God created emotions, and they have no brains. Thoughts, however, fuel emotions, and emotions also influence how and what we think. You can hate a wrong, but it is harder to resist hating the person who wronged you.

Jesus knows how to love those who hate him. Ask him to take the hatred out of your heart and pour his love back into yours. This is a powerful thing to have happen in your life, and it will keep you open with the ability to trust people again.

Hatred keeps you stirred up and stirs up others. Love covers wrongs with such forgiveness that no amount of malice can touch or change the person God created you to be.

DAY 38

So David inquired of the Lord, and he answered, "Do not go straight up, but circle around behind them and attack them in front of the balsam trees. As soon as you hear the sound of marching in the tops of the balsam trees, move quickly, because that will mean the Lord has gone out in front of you to strike the Philistine army." So David did as the Lord commanded him, and he struck down the Philistines all the way from Gibeon to Gezer.

—2 Samuel 5:23–25

David was a great soldier, fighter, and leader. But perhaps his greatest strength was his willingness to follow God. Philistines were bullies that Israel and David had to contend with on a regular basis. David learned that, if he trusted God, he, not David, would deal with his enemy. So before fighting the battle that David knew would have to be fought, he inquired of the Lord first.

Fight-or-flight is a normal reaction when attacked or threatened. But David knew his best course of action, when faced with an army of bullies, was to pray, listen, watch, and move on God's cue. That is exactly what he did.

God's army would be marching on the tops of the trees. When the branches began to move, it meant God's troops had already gone out to fight the Philistines. David was to circle around behind his enemy, but in front of the trees where God's angels would already be fighting. The Lord, David's general, then said, "Move quickly." Because David was ready to move when God told him to, he had victory from one place to another.

Bullies will not stop until they are made to stop. But moving too soon or shrinking back gives them the advantage. Ask God for his plan and when to make a move, and then follow your general "quickly!" Every time you hear the rustling in the treetops, imagine you are hearing him whisper, "The Lord has gone out in front of you."

> God is moving, always moving,
> Fighting battles no one sees,
> Mustering courage in my heart,
> Rustling in the trees.

DAY 39

Starting a quarrel is like breaching a dam; so drop
the matter before a dispute breaks out.

—Proverbs 17:14

Have you ever built a sand castle by the ocean shore? You probably remember digging a deep moat or a trench around your fortress for protection. The higher the tide got, the deeper and more determined you began to dig at that moat! But no matter how hard you tried, your little canal was no match for the ocean. The illusion that you could hold back that avalanche of moving water became apparent when suddenly one giant wave broke over the ditch. It washed away all your hard work. Your palace dissolved into a million grains of sand. But you probably weren't too devastated because that's what waves do and you still had the ability to build another one any time you wanted.

Useless arguments break out when animosity and pride erode away reason and empathy. Like those relentless waves pulling away at your sand structure, so bullies just keep trying to whittle away at anything reasonable you try to say. When caustic people push their opinions and demand you listen while they attack, remember, you don't have to stay there and take it. In other words, don't keep digging your moat! Avoid the trap of arguing with someone who won't stop. Next time you are in that situation, remember the waves on the beach that just kept coming. Take a very deep breath and tell yourself, "Reason just got washed away. Time for me to take a long walk on my beach (or imaginary beach)!"

One of the best arguments you will ever win with bullies is the one you refuse. Nothing deflates the ego of bullies as much as a quarrel you won't give them!

Bully Warning
Though you have an argument
And cruel words you want to say,
I have no time to listen
And no reason to stay.

DAY 40

So do not fear, for I am with you; do not be
dismayed, for I am your God. I will strengthen you
and help you; I will uphold you with my righteous
right hand.

—Isaiah 41:10

Have you ever seen trapeze artists at work? It is a rare sight today. They were the attraction in circus tents years ago, flying high above the crowds. One gymnast swung on bars, doing flips and letting go in midair as another would swing out, reach, and grab tight the acrobat's wrists before he or she had time to drop.

I never enjoyed watching the trapeze artists unless they used a safety net below them. But most acts would not use a net simply for the suspense and risk that drew people to watch. No net meant that one mistimed swing of the bar or slip of the hand and someone was going to die. The high-flying athletes had to be vigilant and trustworthy, each one able to rely on the strong hand and care of the other, day after day. Otherwise, they would be afraid and reluctant to even climb that ladder to the platform.

You also take risks in life. They may not look as dramatic to an outsider, but you feel the sense of danger when stepping out of the house, knowing bullies are looking for you. But once a decision is made not to allow bullies to have control, it is like training for that trapeze event. You have a single focus, determination, and a plan for what you have to do.

That moment in time, when you resolve to no longer be bullied, might be uneasy. Knowing your bullies don't want you standing up to them means that confronting or moving away is going to infuriate them more. Much of the fear subsides once you make a pact with yourself that your life is worth protecting and you are going to take good care of it. When you stand firm and are willing to back them down or get support from dependable people to help you, it is like putting your life into the Master's hands and taking all power out of theirs.

You may not see God's hand reaching out to catch you many times until the last moment, like the trapeze expert, when everything depends on him. Prepare for your part: rid yourself of fear, and make your move. Don't look down. Instead look up and put your faith in the hands of the one that will not let go.

Hold On

Hold on, Lord. I give you my hand.
You have never yet let go.
I'll reach in faith, feel your strong grip,
And trust the God I know.

APPENDIX

BOOKS

Note: Adult, adolescent, and children's books are listed below. Review and choose those that are most appropriate and meet your needs.)

- *The Book on Bullies:* How to Handle Them Without Becoming One of Them by Susan K. Boyd MS, MFT (hardcover, paperback, and eBook)
- *A Bully's Dream: How I Overcame and How You Can Too* by Nick Vujicic
- *Life Without Limits* by Nick Vujicic
- *Adventures in Odyssey: Bothersome Bullies* by Tyndale
- *Woof Tales & Bullies (In a Nic of Time)* by Carol Foster Clark
- *It All Matters to Jesus Devotional for Boys: Bullies, Bikes and Baseball … He Cares About It* by Glen Hascall
- *Buddies Not Bullies Rule!* by Andree Tracey (coloring book)
- *Sorry I'm Not Sorry: An Honest Look at Bullying from the Bully* by Nancy Rue (eBook)
- *Pickles and the P-Flock Bullies* by Stephen Cosgrove
- *Trouble With Bullies* by Gail Wisdom (eBook)
- *Jake Drake, Bully Buster: Ready for-Chapters* by Andrew Clements (eBook)
- *Freda Stops a Bully* by Stuart J. Murphy

- *I Can Speak Bullies* by Jake Maddox
- *Bullies Never Win* by Margery Cuyler
- *Bullying: Bully No More (Hope for the Heart)* by June Hunt (paperback and Kindle eBook)
- *Whipping Boy* by Allen Kurzweil
- *So Not Okay* by Nancy Rue
- *No More Bullies* by Frank E. Peretti
- *God I Need To Talk to You about Bullying* by Susan K. Leigh

WEBSITE

- www.susankboymft.com, author's official site
- stopbullying.gov, official anti-bullying site
- http://www.pacer.org/bullying/resources/info-facts.asp, Pacer's National Bullying Prevention Center, bullying information and facts
- http://bullypolice.org/help_for_parents.html, Bully Police

YOUTUBE VIDEOS

- "Never Ever" by Pacer's National Bullying Prevention Center
- "Don't Laugh at Me" (music video version) with Mark Wills
- They Ask 5 Boys Why 1 Student is A Bullying Victim
- "When You Have to Deal with Bullies"
- "Jock Saved Helpless 'Nerd' From Being Bullied, 4 Years Later He Learned The Heart Wrenching Truth," Inspire More, March 30, 2016
- "Who Will Stop The Bully?"
- "Bully Video"
- "Break The Chain," stopbullying.gov

MUSIC

Note: Down through the ages, music has brought comfort and courage to people. Choose the songs that inspire you to *break free from bullies*.

MUSIC FOR ADOLESCENTS AND ADULTS

Note: Some songs may also, be appropriate and helpful to children

- "Stronger" by Building 429
- "Earth Shaker" by Building 429
- "We Won't Be Shaken" by Building 429
- "Impossible" by Building 429
- "Eyes Up" by Building 429
- "Miss Invisible" by Marie Digby
- "Don't Laugh at Me" by Brad Paisley
- "Hey Bully" by Morgan Frazier
- "Mean" by Taylor Swift
- "Hope in Front of Me" by Danny Gokey
- "Tell Your Heart to Beat Again" by Danny Gokey
- "It's Not Over" by Danny Gokey
- "Giants Fall" by Francesca Battistelli
- "Choose to Love" by Francesca Battistelli
- "If We're Honest" by Francesca Battistelli
- "Run to Jesus" by Francesca Battistelli
- "It's Your Life" by Francesca Battistelli
- "I Know You Can" by Third Day
- "I'm A Survivor" by Destiny's Child
- "Stronger" by Kelly Clarkson
- "Overcomer" by Mandisa
- "Press On" by Mandisa

- "What Scars Are For" by Mandisa
- "Where You Begin" by Mandisa
- "At All Times" by Mandisa
- "Coat of Many Colors" by Dolly Parton
- "Mighty to Save" by Jeremy Camp
- "Same Power" by Jeremy Camp
- "Gold" by Britt Nicole
- "He Is with Us" by Love & Overcome
- "Lift Up Your Head" by Meredith Andrews
- "This Life" by MercyMe
- "The Hurt & The Healer" by MercyMe
- "Last One Standing" by MercyMe
- "Safe and Sound" by MercyMe
- "Greater" by MercyMe
- "New Lease on Life" by MercyMe
- "God's Not Dead (Like a Lion)" by the Newsboys
- "That's How You Change the World" by the Newsboys
- "Defensive Offender" by John Rueben (Rap)
- "Beautiful" by Christina Aguilera
- "Sticks and Stones" by Aly & AJ
- "Hero" by Mariah Carey
- "Fear Not" by Chris Tomlin
- "Impossible Things" by Chris Tomlin (featuring Danny Gokey)
- "Chain Breaker" by Zach Williams
- "It's Not Over Yet" by For King & Country
- "Ceasefire" by For King and Country
- "Fix My Eyes" by For King and Country
- "Steady" by For King and Country

Music For Children

- "Let Yourself Shine (Forget About the Bullies)" by Kore
- "Coat of Many Colors" by Dolly Parton

- "Don't Laugh at Me" by Brad Paisley
- "Mean" by Taylor Swift
- "Hey Bully" by Morgan Frazier
- "Be A Friend Don't Be A Bully" by Jack Hartmann

NOTES

All Bible verses used, unless otherwise specified, were taken from the New International Version Study Bible (Grand Rapids: Zondervan Corporation, 1995).

All website information was current as of March 1, 2017.

All one-page quotes attributed to individuals and introducing chapters can be found on Brainyquote.com.

PART I

CHAPTER 1

1   Matthew Gladden, PhD, et al., (Compilation [2014]), "Bullying Surveillance Among Youths: Uniform Definitions for Public Health and Recommended Data Elements," Centers for Disease Control and Prevention, Atlanta, Georgia, United States, Department of Education, Washington, DC, 4.
2   Ibid., 7–8.
3   "California," http://www.bullypolice.org/ca-law.html.
4   "Cyberbullying Research Center," http://www.cyberbullying.us
5   Ibid.
6   Ibid.
7   Ibid.
8   Ibid.
9   Ibid.

10 "Federal Policy," http://www.olweus.org/public/bullying_laws.page.

11 "California Anti-Bullying Laws & Policies," http://www.stopbullying.
    gov/laws/california.html.

12 "School Security Trends," http://www.schoolsecurity.org/trends/
    bullying.html.

13 "How Do Anti-Bullying Laws Translate to School Policies? Some
    Insights from Washington, D.C.," http://www.huffingtonpost.com/
    Deborah-temkin/how do-anti-bullying-laws_b_6015880.html.

14 http://www.usnews.com/news/articles/2013/09/13/study-antibullying-
    programs-may-have-opposite-effect.

15 Ibid.

16 "Are Anti-Bullying Efforts Making It Worse?", http://www.cbsnews.
    com/news/are-anti-bullying-efforts-

17 Nancy Willard, MS, JD, "Embrace Civility in the Digital Age,
    Influencing Positive Peer Interventions, A *Synthesis of the Research
    Insight* (October 2012), 4–5.

18 Ibid., 5–6.

19 Stan Davis and Julia Davis, *Empowering Bystanders in Bullying Prevention*
    (Champaign, Ill.: Research Press, 2007).

20 Willard, "Embrace Civility in the Digital Age, Influencing Positive Peer
    Interventions," 6.

21 Ellen Pinkos Cobb, Esq., *The Workplace Bullying: A Global Health and
    Safety Issue*, (Boston, Mass., Isosceles Group, 2012).

CHAPTER 2

1 Susan K. Boyd, MS, MFT, *The Book on Bullies: How to Handle Them
   Without Becoming One of Them* (Bloomington, Ind.: WestBow Press,
   2012), 1–28.

2 Allen Kurzweil, *The Forty-Year Search for My Twelve-Year-Old Bully*
   (New York: HarperCollins, 2015).

3 "How Bullied Children Grow Into Wounded Adults," http://
   greatergood.berkeley.edu/article/item.bullied_children_grow_into_
   wounded_adults.

4 "Effects of Bullying," http://www.stopbullying.gov/at-risk/effects/-bully.

5 "Narcissus mythology," Greekmythology.com

CHAPTER 3

1   YouTube Today Show Katie Couric, first interview with Lizzie Velasquez, woman called "World's Ugliest Woman" Becomes Inspiration to All.

CHAPTER 4—BE BOLD, NOT TIMID

1   Susan K. Boyd MS, MFT, *The Book On Bullies: How to Handle Them Without Becoming One of Them* (Bloomington, IN: WestBow Press, 1012), 6-10.

CHAPTER 6

1   *Night Crossing* (1982), Walt Disney Productions.
2   *Bridge of Spies* (2015), DreamWorks.
3   Fredrick Taylor, *The Berlin Wall: A World Divided, 1961–1989* (New York: HarperCollins, 2006), 396.
4   Ibid., 411.
5   Ibid., 410.
6   *Timothy Hughes: Authentic Original Newspapers For Sale.com*

CHAPTER 7

1   S. Hinduja and J. W. Patchin, "Social Influences on Cyberbullying Behaviors Among Middle and High School Students," *J. Adolescents* 42 (5)(2013): 711–722.
2   R. Webster, "From Cyber-bullying to Sexting: What's On Your Kid's Cell?"
3   Kathryn Brohl, MA, LMFT, *Identifying and Addressing Cyber Bullying,* California Mental Health Professionals, EliteCME, 2017 Edition, 121.
4   Ibid.
5   Ibid.
6   Ibid.

Chapter 10

1   13 Celebs You'd Never Guess Were Bullied As Kids, suggest.com
2   Brainyquote, louholtz
3   Brainyquote.com
4   Brainyquote, michaeljordon
5   Brainyquote.com
6   www.notablebiographies.com, Mo-Ni, Napoleon
7   shortfamousmen, huffingtonpost.com
8   15 Famous and Successful People Who Were Bullied in School, Dr. Michael Borba

Chapter 12

1   www.timtebow.com
2   YouTube, Tim Tebow
3   Nick Vujicic, *Life Without Limbs* (Colorado Springs: WaterBrook Press, 2010), 17.

Part II—40 Devotionals to Fortify Your Soul

Day 1

1   Laura Hillenbrand, *Seabiscuit: An American Legend* (New York: The Random House Publishing Group, 2001), 34.

Morro Rock in Morro Bay, California

Susan Boyd is a Licensed Marriage and Family Therapist in private practice in San Luis Obispo, California. She has been married to her husband Jerry for over forty-eight years. They have a son, daughter-in-law, granddaughter, and grandson. Susan says that her favorite activities are spending time with family and friends, writing, engaging in amateur photography, studying the Bible, kayaking, and (occasionally) *trying* to surf. She states she "loves the rugged beauty of the Central Coast." Though she calls Morro Bay home, she still claims dual citizenship with Bakersfield, her hometown.

Printed in the United States
By Bookmasters